A COMPLETE GUIDE ⌐OR GOLFERS OVER 50

How to Reach Your Full Playing Potential and Have Fun Doing It

Presented by Team Golfwell

Published by: Pacific Trust Holdings NZ Ltd., 2018

This book is intended for ADULTS ONLY as there are adult golf jokes, coarse language, and adult stories in this book that the reader, particularly women, may find objectionable.

The book contains exercise programs and diet suggestions. DISCLAIMER: Do the exercises and diet suggestions at your own risk. This Book gives general educational and health-related information and is intended for healthy adults. This information is not and should not be relied on as professional or physical medical advice, diagnosis, or treatment.

This book is solely for general information and educational purposes and does not constitute medical advice. Please consult a medical or health professional before you begin any program in this book for exercise, nutrition, fitness, drills, diet program, or other programs in this book.

There may be risks associated with participating in activities in this book for people who have a health condition or with pre-existing physical or mental health conditions, and you should get a professional medical opinion on whether any of the activities in this book are right for you.

Participating in any exercise or exercise program, always involves the possibility of physical injury, heart attack, stroke, or other problems, especially for people over 50 years of age.

If you engage in any activities or exercises, or anything in this book, you understand and agree that you do so at your own risk, and agree you are voluntarily participating in these activities, assuming all risk of injury to yourself.

Because individuals differ, results will differ.

We are not a licensed medical care provider or dieticians, or health care providers, and represent we have no expertise in diagnosing, examining, or treating medical conditions of any kind, or in determining the effect of any specific exercise on a medical condition or your physique, or nutrition.

Exercise programs are inherently dangerous and if you experience faintness, dizziness, pain, or shortness of breath at any time while exercising you should stop immediately.

If you have any concerns or questions about your physical or mental or general health, you should always consult with a physician or other healthcare professional. Don't disregard, or delay obtaining medical advice from your healthcare professional because of something you may have read in this book.

There are developments in medical research impacting the health, fitness and nutritional advice that appears here. No assurance is given that the advice or anything contained in this book will include the most recent findings or developments with respect to the material.

Thank you to Everkinetic for the images.

The explanations of golf techniques are explained from the point of view of a right-handed golfer. Left-handed golfers should do the opposite.

The adult jokes and adult humorous stories are fictitious.

Praises received:

"I liked this all-encompassing book because of the amount of valuable information in it. I liked the motivation, health aspects, golf tips and techniques, equipment suggestions, exercise programs, diet information, and much more. Thank you, Golfwell, and keep these coming."   - Mary Martin, Orlando

"Enjoyed the book and highly recommend it! I was surprised at the mass of good information in this book for senior golfers. I changed my grip with my left two middle fingers holding the club, and this works well since I hit the ball straight more than I used to."   - Billy Middleton, Las Vegas

"Great last chapter on how to have more fun playing golf. I enjoyed the social aspects, golf games, and humorous aspects of this book. This book makes golf more enjoyable, and I look forward to playing twice a week. I refer to it from time to time. It keeps me positive about life as the years go by. That's what it really is all about." - Don Brice, Lorain, OH

WHY THIS BOOK IS DIFFERENT

This guide is for senior golfers who want to learn a higher level of play and maintain that level as the years pass.

It's also for senior golfers who are looking to have more enjoyment and fun playing golf.

With over 300 pages of golf advice, tips, techniques, equipment advice, ways to loosen stiff joints, complete exercise programs, diet information, fun formats, and much more, this book is a treasury of good information for golfers over 50, and a one stop information source on how to better and maintain your golf skills, and how to really enjoy the game.

You will get motivated after reading this book to play golf to your full potential.

You will learn what Arnold, Jack, Bernhard Langer, Hale Irwin, Trevino, and many other top golfers have said about golfers over 50.

You will get fun golf formats such as "Me Toos," "Wolf for High Handicappers."

You will have our favorite adult jokes and stories to tell during delays on the course, backups at the tee, or the 19th hole clubhouse drinks.

You will get our favorite fitness programs covering the 5 elements needed for a well-rounded fitness program to make you leaner and stronger:

1. Cardio Programs, so you will be less tired during the last 4 to 5 holes.

2. Total Body Resistance and Weight Training. Having good muscle tone makes you play better. Toned muscles use up more calories to help you with weight loss.

3. Core Exercises. You will discover how to strengthen your core muscles to play better, swing easier, and hit it farther.

4. Balance Training. To help you make an even tempo balanced golf swing.

5. Stretching Programs to help maintain your flexibility.

You will learn the diets of top senior golfers.

You will learn why golfers live longer.

Bonus: This book contains a Free Journal to use and keep track of your exercise programs to maintain your fitness.

Read on and begin your journey to your full golf potential by becoming a more skillful, leaner, energetic, and happier golfer!

"Let us never know what old age is. Let us know the happiness time brings and not count the years."

- Ausonius

Contents

1. MOTIVATION: GOLF IS GOOD FOR YOUR HEALTH

Why Golfers live longer

Life is short. Dr. Murray, at the University of Edinburgh, found golfers live longer than people who don't golf since his research team proved those who play golf improve their cholesterol levels, overall health, their own self-esteem, and their own self-worth.[1]

Dr. Murray found the sport of golf showed many health improvements for people no matter what their age may be.[2]

A Swedish study found golfers live longer. This study showed those people who played golf on average lived for five years longer than those who didn't golf.[3]

Padraig Harrington and Annika Sorenstam are both part of the World Golf Foundation's project of scientific research which studies how golf helps, and benefits people to live longer lives.

Padraig and Anika give their support to this World Organization to show they feel playing golf helps people stay fit, active, and healthy.

Dr. Donald Kuah, a well-known sports and exercise physician with Sydney Sports Med Specialists, found there were many health benefits for those that play golf. He found clear evidence that golf increases your lifespan.[4]

Muscle mass decreases as we age, and Dr. Kuah proved that golf is a very good way to improve muscle strength as well as preventing falls.[5]

Keeping your muscles toned increases your metabolism. "As we age, we lose muscle mass, which decreases metabolism, so establishing a strength program will not only increase muscles, it will boost metabolism."[6] Increasing your metabolism contributes to healthy weight loss.

Dr. Ahlbom, a Senior Professor of Epidemiology (the study of healthy living), and former Visiting Scientist in the Department of Epidemiology, Harvard University, believes golf benefits your health. His studies include researching the impact of environmental and lifestyle factors on risks of disease, cancer, and cardiovascular disease.

Dr. Ahlbom said, "Golf involves the outdoors for four or five hours, and walking at a fast pace for several miles, which is all conducive and known to be good for the health."[7]

Dr. Ahlbom's research found the social and psychological benefits of playing golf are very beneficial to your overall well-being.[8]

There are many important things in life, and we asked Gallup about world views on what most people consider the most important thing in life. Most people felt in 2017, having a good job was number one. Second was maintaining good health as a number one priority in life.[9]

Golf helps maintain good relationships, provides an avenue to meet new people, and forms new and strengthens present relationships. The occasional delays on the golf course give you time to interact and bond. We've all seen and know that new business opportunities, and new employment possibilities, are arranged on the golf course, or the 19th hole with follow-up during business hours.

Playing golf burns calories, keeps your heart rate up, reduces stress and makes you sleep better, all of which are benefits to good health.

So, no matter how you play golf, whether you are the Club Champion, or have the highest handicap at your club, find peace and enjoyment in knowing you're on track to maintaining good health.

A golfer decided to have a complete physical examination at a well-known clinic to get himself completely checked out.

After two days of tests, he met with the physician in charge who told him he was doing "fine" for his age.

Concerned about what "fine" meant, he asked the doctor, "Do you think I'll live to reach 85?"

The doctor replied, "Do you smoke cigarettes or fine cigars, drink brandy and fine wines, or any kind of alcohol?"

"Nope." The golfer replied.

"Do you eat filet mignon steaks, fried chicken, bacon and cheese omelets, or barbequed ribs?"

"No, I avoid those foods." The golfer replied.

"Do you spend a time in the sunshine, playing golf, or at the beach, or boating?"

"No, I don't," the golfer replied.

"Do you chase women, go to casinos, or the horse track?"

"No, I don't do any of that, hell, I haven't ever done any of that!" The golfer said.

The doctor studied his charts, then looked at the golfer and said, "Then why do you give a shit if you live to be 85?"

2. WHAT GREAT PLAYERS IN GOLF HAVE SAID ABOUT SENIOR GOLFERS

"It's hard to tell yourself, you don't hit it like you used to, since doing that is nearly impossible."

"But, that shouldn't stop you from trying to hit the ball where you used to hit it, and to make the putts you used to make all the time."

- Arnold Palmer

If you began playing golf in your early years, and if you have a strong character, you will welcome the challenge to maintain and improve your golf ability as you grow older. If you are retired, you may have more time now to learn how to play better.

Arnold Palmer

Arnie kept a positive attitude by setting realistic goals for himself. Arnie believed senior golfers should have a never give up and positive attitude.

Senior golfers can learn a lot from Arnie. Arnie had a simple pre-shot routine where he would first align the clubface behind the ball along the path he wanted it to start out on.

Next, he'd plant his feet and set his feet in a comfortable position making sure the ball was properly placed in his stance to get the trajectory he wanted the ball to fly on.

Then he'd check to see if his feet and shoulders were lined up with the target.

In his pre-shot routine, Arnie had a well-known waggle that kept him loose and eased any tension. He would waggle the club over the ball several times before hitting it.

During the waggles, he would also be adjusting his grip, making small corrections to his grip until it felt right. Then he'd hit the ball when he was ready and although it sometimes seemed unorganized by today's regimented pre-shot routines, Arnie did his waggling very consistently and was very successful at it.

Arnie was always a gentleman, and he wouldn't give up. "I try to win, even when the odds were against me. I always tried."

"I always believed I had a chance to win." Arnie said.

When Arnie putted, he kept perfectly still and held his breath. His only moving parts were his arms and hands.

If he overshot the hole by three feet, he wasn't shy on the second putt. "Many golfers have to fight off tensing up when they hit their second putt after putting it too far past the hole," Arnie said. "You know the line, so hit the second putt firm and smooth, without hesitation."

Arnie said to always try, if possible, to leave your second putt as an uphill putt. He pointed out that "An uphill putt has the back of the cup as a backstop. A downhill putt is just the opposite and has less chance of going in the hole."

Arnie used an old-fashioned barber pole (with red, white, and blue stripes turning in a spiral) as a reminder to turn on an axis when swinging. He'd keep his knees slightly bent and would twist his upper body (without swaying), and then uncoil and make good contact with the ball.

If he found himself swinging too fast and missing his target, Arnie said, "My best cure for swinging too fast is I try to concentrate on getting the club back deliberately away from the ball bringing the club back *slowly for the first few inches*."

When Arnie wasn't making good contact with the ball, he said, "If I want to make good contact, I keep my head still, plant my feet firmly, keep my balance, and get comfortable."

Arnie recommends taking the club away "in one piece, without breaking your wrists" for at least a foot when driving the golf ball. "This will get your upper body turning," Arnie said.

Arnie also believed an amateur golfer should putt rather than chip when you can cleanly hit the ball from off the green to the pin. "Even the worst putt you do will most of the time be better than your best chip."

Arnie said, "If you don't believe me, try putting 10 balls from off the green, then chip 10 balls from the same spot off the green, and you'll see what I mean."

For chipping, Arnie recommended you brush the grass with the clubhead like you were sweeping the ball off the grass on its way toward the pin.

On sand shots, Arnie would keep his legs quiet with knees bent. He'd swing with his arms only which kept him from swaying or moving up or down on the shot. "Using just arms made my sand shots more consistent and made it easier for the leading edge of the clubhead to enter the sand in the exact spot I wanted it to."

Arnie made sure he had the right grip. He'd take his time placing his left hand on the club, having it cross the palm of his left hand, and he checked to make sure he was using the grip he wanted to for the shot he was about to hit. Then he would just add his right hand on the grip, once his left hand was positioned correctly.

Jack Nicklaus

Some players tend to give up on a hole when things go bad. Jack Nicklaus said, "Don't ever quit, don't give up, no matter what."

Jack is telling us having an attitude of "Not giving up" will get you back on track. He said, "You should positively believe you can play a shot. Don't start thinking and wondering when the next bad shot is coming."

Emotions get in the way of golf. We knew a young golfer whose father kept encouraging him to play professional golf. But he kept missing cuts for opportunities to qualify for pro tournaments. One day he finally qualified for a PGA Tour Event. He was only 22 years old at the time and had his dad caddy for him.

He did well in the Pro-Am on Wednesday, but the excitement of playing in his first PGA Tour event got into his head on the first tee on Thursday, and he hit his first tee shot on the first hole out of bounds.

He took a deep breath and teed up another ball, then hit his second drive out of bounds as well. "Then it got worse from there on out," he told us.

He later became a Club Pro, and eventually owned and operated a large driving range, sold it, and is now enjoying a successful retirement.

If you are in a serious competition, the club championship, or even a $2 Nassau, keep a cool head and stay positive and focused.

Seniors can learn a lot from how Jack played. Jack's pre-shot routine is simple and remained the same during his entire playing career. He would stand behind the ball and survey his surroundings taking in all the factors important to him, then he would focus on a specific target and visualize how to hit the ball there.

Jack was excellent at managing a golf course. He said to be successful at golf, there are two things to master when you play, "The golf course and yourself."

"Golf is a game of being exact as you can, and it's not a game of strength," Jack said.

Even if Jack was hitting it badly, his course management skills made him win, "A big part of managing a golf course is managing your swing on the course. You have to think about where you want to hit it, and how you are going to get the ball there."

Hale Irwin said, "Jack thought his way around the golf course better than anyone else."

Going back to his pre-shot routine, Jack would discuss the yardage with his longtime caddy, Angelo Argea, then visualize the shot, and select a club to hit it to his target.

Jack was consistent. He kept his pre-shot routine, swing, etc. the same over the years. He shaped his well-thought-out shots with exact precision.

Alignment: Jack would select a specific target, then draw a line back from his target to his ball selecting a blade of grass or spot about 3 to 4 feet in front of him in direct line with his target.

He would take his stance, and he would turn his left foot slightly outward. Then, he'd take one or two waggles with his club, as a reminder to stay loose.

When he was ready to hit the ball, he triggered each swing by first turning his chin about an inch or two to the right, before turning his shoulders, arms, and club to begin the swing.

Jack said he avoids pressure while playing. "If you concentrate, you take away the pressure. Don't make excuses after bad shots. That will make you feel more pressure. I try not to do that."

Frank Beard, a competitor to Jack said, "The mental side? Nicklaus was the best. He was organized and maintained his discipline and composure. I never saw him lose his cool."

Gary Koch said, "Jack was always on an even keel. That allowed his mind to work at its best. Jack had great emotional stability."

Jack said he didn't have a pre-putt routine. He took his time until he felt comfortable. Jack needed to get a "feel" for the putt before he'd hit it. Jack crouched (almost stood hunchbacked) to visualize the line of a putt. He did this since he knew he was left-eye dominant. Crouching with an open stance, made it easier for him to see the line of the putt with his left eye. "It was the only way I could see the line," Jack said.

Johnny Miller perhaps put it best, "Jack's not a normal competitor. He's the only guy I know who is actually pleased to see someone make birdies. That pushes him to play better. He has great discipline."

Tiger Woods

Seniors can learn a lot from Tiger Woods. Tiger explained his pre-shot routine is what he personally likes, and other pros have different pre-shot routines.

If wind is a factor, he will first toss blades of grass in the air testing and studying wind direction and force.

He takes a full view of the intended target, and the trouble around the target such as bunkers, water, trees, etc. He discussed the yardage with his long-time caddy, Steve Williams, and other points, e.g. bunkers or other hazards, etc., as talking about the shot you are about to hit takes pressure off.

If he's going for the pin, he'll get the exact yardages involved on everything around the green, e.g. yardages on bunkers, lakes, front of green, back of the green, etc. Then he visualizes the shot and decides on the club he wants to use to get the ball there.

Tiger routinely towels off the handle of the club he selects. Then he takes slow practice swings while discussing the shot with his caddie and the yardages.

He stands behind the ball and again, visualizes the shot he's decided upon. He pics a small target and aligns the shot.

He waggles the club and takes two to three full practice swings. After that, he'll take one waggle, and begin to turn just his shoulders, reminding himself to turn his shoulders when he swings.

He'll take one more full practice swing. Then he'll take his stance and look at his target, then he'll look at the ball and hit it.

If he feels uncomfortable, or just wants to take another look at the shot he's about to make, he'll step away and walk behind the ball, and then go through the identical pre-shot routine.

Tiger said he believes in having only one swing thought at a time, but when he putts, he visualizes and thinks about seeing the ball go into the hole.

Tiger was known as one of the greatest putters in golf. He used a pre-putt routine.

When he walked onto the green, Tiger would take in the contour, and the surroundings, then mark his ball. When it was his turn to putt, he replaced the ball and did this 8-step pre-putt routine:

1. First, he walked halfway from his ball to the hole to see the second half of the putt and how it would break - if at all.

2. Next, he did a 360 degree walk around to view the putt from all perspectives, and stopped where he wanted to take in the details, i.e. uphill or downhill, left to right or right to left, etc.

3. During the 360-degree walk around, he stopped at the golf hole and looked down into the golf hole and studied the grain of the green.

4. After completing the walk around, he developed a feel for how the putt would break.

5. He decided on the line, pace and feel of the putt, and took his stance as if he was ready to putt, and then took two practice strokes. He looked up at the hole as he finished the second practice stroke.

6. He then adjusted his feet to get comfortable and placed his putter behind the ball and aligned it to where he wanted it to start out.

7. He looked up once more at the hole.

8. Then hit the putt.

As for being patient, Tiger said, "I do know if I'm patient, it can turn out very well."

Tiger worked out regularly when he was on the tour working out five to six days per week. He stretched for 30 minutes and did high reps with weights (25 to 50 reps). During the high reps, he focused on his balance, control, endurance, and speed.

He changed his routine often varying the angle of the exercises to cover all muscles. He liked strengthening the back muscles, and his upper back shoulder muscles for good posture.

Tiger worked hard practicing at the range, as well as in the gym, and it paid off for him.

Tiger kept a realistic and positive attitude when he played. His goal then, and his goal today is to keep trying to win more major tournaments than anyone, and he knows time is running out.

As people get older, they deal with more issues, worries, problems, aches, and pains. This, of course, creates pressure in trying to perform like you used to on the golf course. Tiger said no matter what your age, it's important to keep a cool head. "I just have the knack for staying on an even keel, and if the situation gets very tense, I tend to see things more clearly."

Bernhard Langer

Seniors can also learn a lot from Bernhard Langer who is now the second-highest all-time money winner on the PGA Champion's Tour. Bernhard carefully maintains his health. He stretches twice a day, and exercises in gyms during his travels on the Champions Tour on a regular basis.

He had a bad back when he was young and said, "I had a history of a bad back. Started when I was 19 - I had two bulging disks, a very bad neck, and a bad lower back…. So, I needed to stretch, I needed to work out and stay fit." And he continued his gym and stretching to this day.

Bernhard said, "When I raise up from the shot too quickly, and don't keep my head still and down, I put more stress on my back."

Langer said raising his head too quickly makes the ball go high and to the right, since his clubface is open when it contacts the ball. When things start going bad during play, check yourself to see if you're raising your head too quickly. Try keeping it still and down after striking the shot and see if that makes a difference.

Angel Cabrera

Angel is 48 years old as of the time of this writing, and will soon be playing the PGA Champions Tour.

Angel was one of the most aggressive competitors on the PGA Tour. Angel believes keeping a "good tempo and rhythm" in a golf swing is essential, especially when the competition is fierce, and the pressure is on.

He looks at getting older in a very positive way. "You should welcome getting older in golf. You know your swing more and knowing your swing will make you keep improving easier than the new golfer."

On the lighter side, although Columbia University Professor Simon Schama is not a golfer, he made a comment about aging and being more active with things other than golf. There may be other sports or activities you want to enjoy – whatever interests you.

He said, "The older I get, the more I want to do." He continued, "Doing a lot of things as you get older beats death, decay, or golf in unfortunate trousers. Peace and quiet depresses me."

That's an interesting philosophy we might want to think about. It gives us motivation to get off the couch as we age and get up or get outdoors and do things.

Greg Norman

Greg Norman believes you should get out and do things too. We contacted his office about his philosophies in life and he told us, "My goal was always to be the best I could be. Trying to be the best you can be has no limit since you have room to grow, something new to learn, and new things to try to do."

Greg totaled 331 weeks ranked as the #1 golfer in the world (only Tiger Woods had more weeks at #1).

Greg doesn't play golf a lot now and said in 2017 he only played about 8 to 10 rounds of golf, mostly with his son.

Greg didn't let losing get to him. Greg has said, "Every time you lose, you tend to think something is unfair. You get bad breaks from nowhere. But, those bad breaks come whether you are playing well or playing bad. They just happen, and you have to keep a strong mind."

Don't quit playing golf if you have reoccurring problems with the game that can be corrected.

Greg has said you need to set goals. "Set a goal for your golf game and the trick in setting goals for yourself is not to set them too high. Set them realistically at a good level – not too low or too high."

Seniors can learn a lot from Greg. His shot strategy was to play the best shot he had the best chance of making and not to overthink shots.

Greg has said about his pre-shot mind, "As I walk between shots, I let my mind wander to all sorts of non-golf things - to my kids, to my next fishing trip, or whatever - but when I'm playing my best, my mind clicks back into focus well before I reach the ball."

Greg has said, "At a point about 40 yards short of the ball I begin to analyze the situation that's facing me. I look at the tops of the trees to check the wind, I look at the pitch and roll of the green area to get an initial feel for the way the ball will roll, and I look at the people around the green to get depth perception. By the time I get to my ball, I'm fully focused on the shot."

"Some of my colleagues on Tour delay this type of thinking until they arrive at the ball. I'm not saying they're wrong, but I do recommend my method to all amateurs, and for one big reason - it will speed up play!"

Have you ever lost the "feel" of putts? You putt well on the first hole, then you lose your feel on the second hole unexplainably?

To avoid losing feel, Greg uses a putting technique which he refers to as "Hold the hold." Many golfers take a practice putting stroke with a relaxed grip and make the practice stroke exactly as they want to hit the putt. They then loosen their grip and regrip the putter too tightly, when they attempt their actual putt.

Greg has said if you make a nice practice putt, don't loosen your grip and "hold the hold" when you make the actual putt. Tom Watson and others used this "hold the hold" method very successfully.

Greg suffered back injuries which made it difficult for him to play on the Champions Tour. Greg turned 50 in February 2005 but has kept his distance from the senior golf circuit due to business demands and his back problems. Greg felt he would have avoided the back injuries had golf fitness been more widely used during his golf career. Greg now spends an hour and a half to two hours daily in his gym.

Nick Faldo

Seniors can learn a lot from Nick Faldo. Nick won 41 professional golf tournaments, including 6 major tournaments (he won the Masters 3 times and the Open 3 times) and was ranked #1 in the world.

Nick simply loved the fascinating game of golf, and the game simply agreed with Nick. Nick later became a successful golf analyst for major broadcasting networks.

For pre-shot routines, he recommends once you've determined the distance and selected your club, the next step is visualization, then alignment, "It's obvious that it is no good having a perfect setup, perfect grip and perfect golf swing if the whole thing is misaligned."

Nick also believes the most important part of his pre-shot routine is the practice swing.

Nick refers to the practice swing as a "Rehearsal" of exactly what you are going to try to do with the shot. He recommends before taking your stance, simulate what you are about to do.

"Don't just look at your target and say to yourself, 'Oh, I just want to hit it about 100 yards,' then go into your stance without a practice swing and hit the ball," said Nick.

Nick does practice swings behind the ball, or next to the ball - wherever he finds it most comfortable. Then he rehearses hitting the shot. "Hit an imaginary ball to your target practicing your swing at the exact tempo you intend to use."

When you do this "Rehearsal", Nick said, "Block anything else completely out of your mind other than what you exactly want to accomplish with this shot."

Then, Nick said, if you feel comfortable, "Step straight in, and hit the shot."

Nick believes if you are blocking everything else than what you are about to do with the shot, and you've rehearsed the shot hitting an imaginary ball, "Your mind adjusts easier from the rehearsal and the real thing."

Tempo is important to Nick, "Tempo is the glue that sticks all elements of the golf swing together."

Nick is fit and watches what he eats, and how much he eats. "If you want to play better, you must eat better, you have to look out for yourself."

When putting, Nick points out it's very important to focus keeping your wrists straight and you must have your hands moving in the direction you want to ball to travel.   "Too many golfers focus on the ball and the putter head to be lined up in the direction you want to go," said Nick.

It's important to be positive on the golf course. Nick said, "A year ago, I looked at a golf course and it was like 18 bear traps. I thought, 'How can I avoid getting my ankles bitten off?'"

"Now I am thinking good thoughts and planning my way around the course. Now I'm thinking, 'Let's make some birdies and see what score I can shoot.'"

You get more positive by allowing yourself to accept bad shots happen, and think good thoughts instead.

Lee Trevino

Lee Trevino has made many jokes about getting older like, "The older I get, the better I used to be."

Lee was born in 1939 and said senior golfers should consider slowing down their golf swing when they want to hit it farther. He said, many seniors want to hit the ball farther, so they consciously or unconsciously swing harder. Making good contact is easier to do if you don't rush your swing.

Lee has recommended just having the thought of making good contact with the ball, is all you need to do, and forget about swinging at it harder.

Lee gracefully accepted growing older. He's positive yet matter-of-fact about life. "I never think of yesterday. Can't do anything about it. I'm a positive guy. When you deep down look at it, we go to bed every night, get up every morning, stay here for 70 or 80 years, and then we die."

Sam Snead

Consistency is hard for senior golfers. Sam Snead has won more professional tournaments than any other player. Sam Snead said consistency is part of the mental game. Sam suggested not to get emotional about shots on the course to be more consistent. "To be consistent, you have to distance yourself from what happens on the golf course. Don't be indifferent to it, just detach yourself and don't let the bad shots get inside you."

When you are working on your game, Sam said, "Correct one fault at a time. Concentrate on the one fault you want to overcome."

Phil Mickleson

Senior golfers can learn a lot from Phil Mickleson. He turned pro after college when he was 21 years old and became a very successful golfer winning 5 major championships.

His pre-shot routine is multi-faceted. He considers many factors on each shot. He first establishes how far he can hit a club under the existing conditions. Let's say he normally hits his 8-iron 160 yards.

Phil knows that the 8 iron/160 yards varies depending on the wind, the temperature, the altitude of the course; and the fact that golf balls travel farther in warmer temperatures so there is a difference playing the colder morning rounds than warmer afternoon rounds on tour.

If he's playing in the morning, there may be dew and water on the ball which Phil knows increases spin and the ball goes shorter.

He considers the lie of the ball. If he's hitting an approach shot to the green, he needs to know the grain of the green, and the slopes on the green. He then determines how he wants the ball to come into the green.

He processes these factors, as well as any other relevant factors, and decides on a club and how he is going to hit the shot. Phil said, taking all the factors into account is very important. "That's why I've been known to be such an accurate iron player."

Phil hasn't ever won a U.S. Open but came in second twice. He didn't play the 2017 U.S. Open which surprised many people since winning the US Open is something he wanted very much to accomplish in his career. Phil passed up the 2017 U.S. Open so he could be at his daughter's high school graduation, where she gave the valedictorian speech.

Phil takes in many factors when putting as well. Phil's best putting tip is to make sure your putter head is properly aligned with the path you want the ball to take. "You can have the most beautiful putting stroke, but the stroke itself is minor. Consistent setup, reading greens and aiming the putting face is more important."

Hale Irwin

As of the time of this writing, Hale Irwin is the highest money winner on the PGA Champions Tour. He has a positive attitude about golf competitions. "If you find yourself thinking too much on bad shots, you're being negative. I don't like that. I'd rather be positive and think about the things I did well."

Hal said to take care of yourself and you'll play better. Hal said if you become tired and start hitting bad shots, "The best thing to do is to focus on your rhythm and balance."

Hal has a keen insight into the individual sport of golf, and he went on record encouraging everyone to keep playing. "Golf brings out the best in yourself, and the worst in yourself personally. If you've been playing golf a long time you know that the performance of a golfer shows who he really believes he truly is."

Bobby Jones

The great Bobby Jones who retired from golf at the age of 28 believed the golf swing should be relaxed. "Being comfortable and relaxed during the golf swing is key and you establish it in the address position."

In 1960, the concept of a pre-shot routine wasn't as common as it is today. Bobby believed every golfer needs to standardize the approach to every shot, and it should begin even before you address the ball.

Many older golfers don't do a pre-shot routine, or sometimes older golfers overthink each shot. Bobby wrote, "The more I fiddled around arranging the position, the more I was beset by doubts which produced tension and strain."

To avoid "tension and strain," Bobby suggested a simple pre-shot routine:

1) "I began to approach every shot from behind the ball looking towards the hole."

2) "I would stop a little short of what my final stance position would be - just near enough to the ball to reach it comfortably."

3) "From there, the club was grounded, and I took one look towards the objective."

4) "One waggle was begun while the right foot moved to its place. When the club returned to the ground behind the ball, there was a little forward twist of the hips, and the backswing began."

Bobby said not to take more than one waggle. "Whenever I hesitated or took a second waggle, I could look for trouble."

The "forward twist of his hips" was necessary to Bobby. "The little twist of the hips is a valuable aid in starting the swing smoothly, because it assists in breaking up any tension which may have crept in."

A swing starter is good for senior golfers to break any tension, since bad shots seem to occur more as we age and creates unnecessary tension.

3. LAUGHTER HELPS YOU LEARN EASIER AND BENEFITS YOUR HEALTH

Adults learn easier when laughter is involved. Laughter makes absorbing new information easier.[10]

Many research projects have proven laughter helps learning. There is a relationship between laughing and learning since laughter tends to make a person lower his defenses, and the result is it's easier to learn new things while you're in good humor.

Golf tips are more easily absorbed and become part of your game when there's laughter involved. You're much more receptive to learning things to help you play better.

Medical research has shown laughter relieves your stress response and a good honest laugh leaves you with a good relaxed feeling.[11]

It's been often said, "It's like hell getting old." It's easy to gradually take on a negative and short-tempered attitude as you grow older.

Playing golf gets you away from the problems and the worries in life, as well as daily stress. It gives you time to relax and enjoy the outdoors, as well as opportunities for laughter and socializing.

Even though we've heard people say, "Missing 3-foot putts can cause brain damage" (we haven't found any evidence of this yet, Haha!), golf is good for your mental health as well, since it adds relaxation and laughter.[12]

When you are relaxed, your muscles aren't tensed up, and your mind becomes clearer, and your brain processes information more easily. The beneficial result is your golfing ability gets better.

If you're under stress, your body releases stress hormones. Laughter reduces these stress hormones in your body since it triggers the release of endorphins, the body's natural feel-good chemicals which produce a sense of feeling good and reduces pain levels.[13]

Medical research has shown laughter will make you think more clearly, break negative thoughts more easily, communicate easier in therapy sessions, makes relationships stronger, and even helps the post-traumatic stress disorder.[14]

According to the US National Institute of Health, "Depression is a disease where neurotransmitters in the brain, such as norepinephrine, dopamine, and serotonin, are reduced, and ... laughter increases the levels of dopamine and serotonin activity."[15]

In addition, laughter therapy helps people get out of a depression even without drugs. Endorphins are released by laughter which helps people become comfortable and escape depression. Laughter therapy is a non-invasive and non-pharmacological alternative treatment for stress and depression. Laughter therapy is effective and scientifically supported.[16]

If you get depressed, try an experiment on yourself. Think back to a time, or times in your life, when you couldn't stop laughing, and dwell and reflect on that time or times in your past for a short while. Then, see if those memories make you feel more relaxed and feeling better overall.

Watch this contagious British laughter video featuring Bradley Walsh, of the Chase TV Quiz

Show, who couldn't stop laughing. See if you experience an overall feeling of well-being and relaxation after watching.[17] If you have the printed version of this book, here is the YouTube link: https://www.youtube.com/watch?v=b28_wgzR34Y

If you find yourself hitting bad shots consecutively during a golf round, think back to a time in your life when you couldn't stop laughing, and reflect on it. Then, see if your shots improve.

Laughter helps build social relationships since it relieves the usual awkward tension when you meet someone for the first time. Laughter makes it much easier to get to know each other.

Psychology today has numerous articles on how laughter benefits relationships, as well as helps form new relationships. One of the best ways to warm up a relationship is laughter. Most everyone desires laughter, and it helps form good genuine relationships.[18]

A good laugh makes learning new golf techniques easier.

4. PRE-ROUND WARM UPS

How to Loosen Stiff Joints Before a Round

Osteoarthritis is the major cause of joint stiffness as cartilage that connects the bones in joints deteriorates as we grow older; and since there is no cure yet for osteoarthritis, the best we can do right now is to manage it.[19] Low impact exercise will help you manage stiffness and joint pain.

The most common way to warm up before starting a golf round is to spend 5 to 10 minutes chipping, 10 to 15 minutes on the range, and 5 to 10 minutes on the putting practice green, before proceeding to the first tee to begin your round.

If you still don't feel ready to begin a round, there might be other causes for your soreness or stiffness, and you should seek medical advice.

Our favorite 8-minute pre-round warm up routine you can do at home, or in the club locker room, is a routine offered free by Fitness Blender https://www.fitnessblender.com/videos/total-body-warm-up-workout-routine

You can put the Fitness Blender Warm-Up-Routine YouTube video on your phone, which would enable you to do this 8-minute warm up routine while waiting on the first tee.

When you watch this 8-minute Fitness Blender Warm-Up video, you will see there is a 60-second rope jumping exercise as the last warm up exercise. Instead of jumping rope, try jogging in place for the last 60 seconds.

Finally, if you don't have the time to warm up, you can still do practice swings with your driver for 5 minutes, or more, before beginning your round of golf. While doing practice swings, concentrate on maintaining an even tempo and swing as smoothly as you can.

Keep your mind clear when doing the practice swings. Don't overswing. Using a consistent and smooth tempo, is far better than swinging as fast and as hard as you can.

If you still feel sore or stiff after the usual warmup, or if you just don't have a lot of time to do a warmup, do these simple exercises and stretches in the following order. This routine takes about 5 to 10 minutes.

If you experience pain while doing any of these, you should stop and get medical advice. Begin by stretching. It's best not to force or bounce any stretch. If you feel pain, stop stretching or don't push your stretch further. Stretch only to the point where you comfortably feel an easy stretch.

Don't hold your breath as you stretch. Breath normally in and out 3 times each as you stretch, and this will make each stretch last about 20 seconds. You should feel very loose after doing all these stretches and exercises and play the round better.

The pre-round loosening up stretch exercises which follow in this Chapter are Knee Circles plus:
- Forearm and Wrist Stretching
- Full Body Stretching (Don't force or push any stretch to the limit – just stretch as far as you comfortably are able)
- Side Bends
- Arm Swings with Toe Touches
- Arm Circles
- Torso Twists, and a few optional exercises.

Knee Circles. If you have no problems with your knees or ankles, do knee circles to loosen up your ankles and knees while waiting on the tee. Begin by standing upright with a slight bend in your knees. Your feet should be flat on the ground and put your hands on your hips, then move your knees in a circular motion for 1 minute. Repeat if needed.

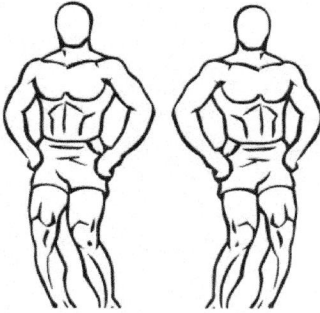

FOREARM AND WRIST STRETCHING. Hold your left arm out in front of you and bend your left hand back with your palm facing forward (don't force it) and hold for 15 seconds.

Repeat the same with your right arm in front.

Next, hold your left arm out and point your fingers to the ground with your palm facing you. Then bend your hand back (don't force it) toward your body and hold for 15 seconds.

Repeat the same with your right arm.

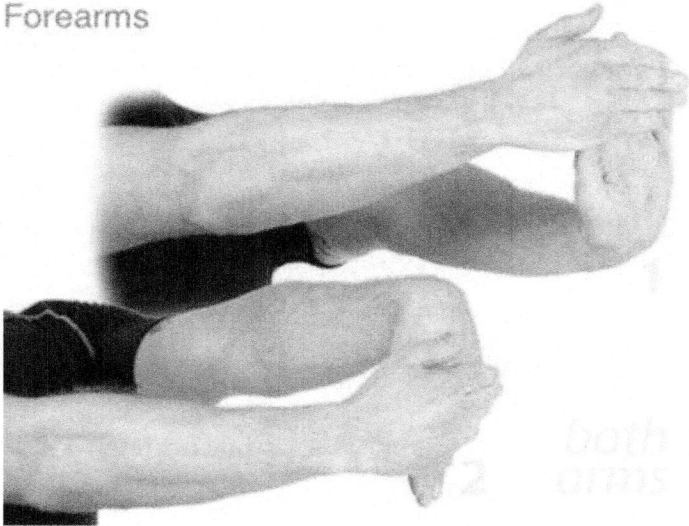

Forearms

FULL BODY STRETCHES. After you've done your forearm and wrist stretches, do as many of the stretches shown in the following diagram as you can, stretching for 20 seconds each. Do this in the locker room or wherever you can.

Again, stretch gradually. If you feel pain, don't stretch any further. Stretch only to the point where you comfortably feel an easy stretch.

Don't hold your breath as you stretch. Breath normally 3 times in and out as you stretch.

You should feel very loose after doing these stretches and play better.

30 seconds each leg

15 seconds each leg

20 seconds each leg

20 seconds each leg

20 seconds each leg

20 seconds each leg

15 seconds each arm

20 seconds

5 seconds each 3 times

20 seconds each side

SIDE BENDS. Do these in a relaxed way and don't force or push the side bends.

Begin in a standing position bending your arms behind your head as shown in the diagram. Bend sideways back and forth from right to left and vice versa. Do 20 complete side bends, bending to each side 10 times each.

Rest 10 seconds and do another set of 20 complete side bends.

You can also begin these exercises by holding a golf club above your head with your arms straight up, instead of folding your arms behind your head.

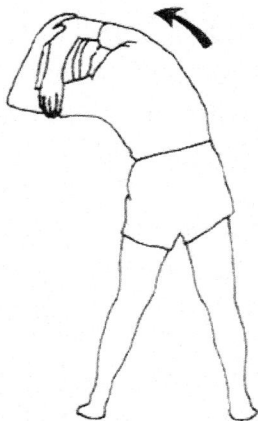

ARM SWING WITH TOE TOUCHES:

Begin in a standing position with feet positioned outside of your shoulders and extend your arms out sideways from your body and perpendicular to the ground.

Bend forward (only bend down as far as you can comfortably), then swing your left arm toward your right shoe and raise your right arm toward the sky.

Do 10 to 15 twists in each direction, keeping your weight in your heels, and a slight bend in your knees. Repeat and do a second set 10 to 15 twists in each direction.

ARM CIRCLES:

Extend your arms out sideways from your body and do arm 20 circles circling your arms forward. Then do arm circles in the opposite direction 20 more times.

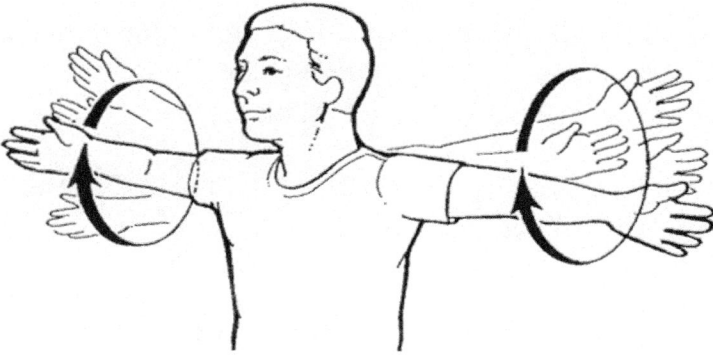

How To Loosen Up the Upper Body

Begin in a standing position with both knees slightly bent and holding a weighted object (5 lbs maximum, or you can do this holding a golf club out in front of you) and twist side to side a total of 20 twists with 10 twists in each direction.

Rest 10 seconds, then do a second set of 20 twists with 10 twists in each direction.

Other Quick Warm Up Exercises:

The following exercises are more rigorous. If you are used to doing these exercises, do them moderately in any amount that you are comfortable with, to get your muscles warmed up:

Squats

Begin in a standing position and extend your arms outward in front of you. You can also do this holding out a golf club in both hands parallel to the ground. If you need support, hold on to a stationary object like a bench or a post.

Lower to a squat position, keeping your back straight and look forward. Squat down only as far as you comfortably can, then raise up to the standing starting position. Do 10 squats and repeat if you want to.

Jumping Jacks, Jog in Place, Burpees

Any of these high intensity cardio exercises will raise your pulse and get blood to the muscles of your body and loosen you up before beginning a golf round.

Do them in moderation for a minute or two only if you are used to doing these exercises.

If you are looking for an exercise program you can do regularly for 3 days a week, and only have about 35 minutes for each session, our favorite routine is Fitness Blender Free Golf Specific 35-minute Exercise Video which is a difficult routine for those over 50. See > https://www.fitnessblender.com/videos/fitness-blender-golf-workout-strength-balance-and-flexibility-exercises-for-golfers if you're curious and in excellent physical condition.

Besides doing these exercises, there are other things you can plan to do to improve your golf game as well as your quality of life:

1. Give your joints adequate rest to relieve pain and adjust any swelling.

2. Lose weight. You don't have to lose a lot of weight. It's been shown just losing a few pounds will help lessen the hip and knee stiffness and pains of osteoarthritis.[20]

5. GOLF TIPS AND TECHNIQUES FOR BETTER SCORING

Driving Techniques For More Distance - Increased Angle of Attack.

Extend your driving distance by 10 to 15 yards by increasing the angle of attack when teeing up the ball.

If you tee the ball forward two to three inches from where you normally tee the ball, your club head will strike the ball on an upward angle.

Justin Thomas with his 150 lb. 5-foot 9-inch frame consistently hits the ball on the upswing when he hits a tee shot. The result is an exceptionally long drive since his clubhead strikes the back of the ball at about a 5-degree upward angle of attack.

Striking the ball off the tee on the upswing causes the ball to fly higher and increase distance.

Avoid over swinging when you tee the ball higher and forward - just swing at your normal speed and focus on making a good smooth swing rather than swinging hard.

Take a normal stance, or even a slightly wider stance to create a bigger arc in your swing and help your stability.

The ball teed up forward may look odd to you. If it looks out of balance, focus on a spot on the ground behind the ball. Or, imagine a ball is teed up in the normal position where you usually tee it up (e.g., off your left heel), and look at a spot on the ground where your normal ball would be teed up.

Then make a smooth swing, disregarding the actual ball is teed up slightly further ahead 2-3 inches. Your club will do the rest and strike the ball on the upswing.

Some golfers find it helpful to look at the back of the ball, while others look at a spot on the ground where they would normally tee the ball.

Here are 5 steps to increasing the angle of attack from our book, "Driving Techniques of Golfing Greats...,"[21]

"1. Angle of Attack: Do a slow practice swing and find your position 2 shown on the following diagram" (note: "Pos. 2 is the lowest point of the arc where the bottom of your clubhead is closest to the ground.").

"In the diagram, the first position is position 1 where the clubhead is traveling on a downward arc. Position 2 is the bottom of the arc, and Position 3 is two to three inches in front of Position 2.

"2. Tee the ball up higher than normal and tee the ball forward to Position 3. This will increase the angle at which the face of the clubhead will be on the upswing and contact the back of the teed-up ball.

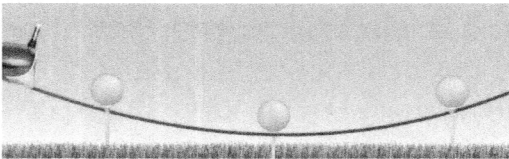

| 1 | 2 | 3 |

"3. Lower your right shoulder (i.e. assuming you are a right-handed golfer) when you take your stance.

"A way to test to see if your right shoulder is lowered enough, is to take your right hand off the grip and let your right arm hang down. You should be able to easily touch the top of your right knee cap with your right hand.

"4. Check to see if the handle of the driver is on an approximate angle of 45 degrees pointing to your midsection (or approximately at your belt line).

"5. Then make your usual swing at your normal swing speed. There is a tendency to swing harder, but it's important to keep your normal tempo and timing when hitting."

Drawing the ball.

Another way to increase distance is to hit a draw tee shot, i.e., a tee shot that curves from right to left.

There are several ways to draw the ball off the tee making it curve from right to left. Balls hit with a draw tend to roll farther in the fairway.

One easy way to hit a draw is to simply close your clubface. The more you close your clubface, the more draw you will create. You must aim to the right of your target and allow for the right to left curve.

Another easy way to hit a draw is to take a closed stance when you address the ball. You close your stance by dropping your right foot back, so your shoulder line is lined up to the right of your club face. The more you drop your right foot back, the more your stance is closed, and the more draw you will create. Closing your club face and closing your stance will create an even larger draw.

If you use either of these methods, remember to swing smoothly with an even tempo, and the ball will go right to left.

Also, play the ball slightly back in your stance from where you normally tee the ball.

Experiment gradually closing your stance on the driving range and determine the amount of draw you generate with each position in varying closed stance degrees you take. Try dropping your right foot back at different distances, ranging from a third of a shoe length back, to a full shoe length back or more.

A closed stance will also open your hips making it easier to turn your hips as you bring the club back.

You can also create a draw by taking a stronger grip which means starting with a neutral grip, then turning your right hand further to the right. You should be able to see either one or two knuckles on your right hand, and one knuckle on your left hand.

Hitting a Power Fade Off the Tee

To hit a fade off the tee, you do the opposite of hitting a draw. There are two ways to hit a fade off the tee which are:

1. Swing normally but open your clubface. The more you open your clubface the more draw you will hit. You aim to the left of your target depending on the amount of fade you are going to hit.

2. Swing normally but address the ball with an open stance. The more your stance is open, the more fade you will hit.

Practice hitting a bucket on the range testing the fade by opening your clubface and by opening your stance.

When you open the clubface point the clubface at the target or slightly to the left of your target. Then open your stance so your shoulders and toe line are aimed further to the left than your clubface.

You can open your stance by advancing your right foot forward in your stance and turning your left foot slightly out. Align your toe and shoulder line to hit further to the left of your clubface.

There are other ways to hit a fade by adjusting your grip.

You adjust your grip to hit a fade by rolling your left hand to the left and right hand to the right. You shouldn't be able to see any knuckles on your left hand. You should only see knuckles on your right hand which should be covering your left thumb.

Lee Trevino, Tiger Woods and others use a power fade by holding the club with three fingers of their left hand to prevent the club face from closing right before striking the ball.

DRILL: Learn to Hit a Power Fade Tee Shot

At the range, pick a target directly ahead of you – i.e., straight ahead at the 12 o'clock position.

Place the ball on the tee with the brand of the ball (or line up a straight line marked on the ball) pointing to the 12 o'clock position.

If you want more fade, point the brand of the ball (or straight line marked on the ball) to the 11:00 or 11:30 o'clock position, i.e., to the left of the target allowing for the fade.

Open your stance by advancing your right foot forward and line up your toe and shoulder line pointing to the 10:00 or 10:30 o'clock position.

Point the club face to the 11:00 or 11:30 position, i.e., slightly to the left of your target.

Use your normal swing and you will fade the ball.

Also, tee the ball up on the right side of the tee and the fairway will look larger to you.

Practice fading the ball on the range by adjusting the amount of opening your clubface and opening your toe and shoulder line to the left in your stance. Your toe and shoulder line should line up left of your target and left to where your clubface is pointing.

Take Away Wide in One Piece

You can increase distance if you tee the ball up and imagine the clubhead of your diver is aligned and parallel to the top rail of a railroad track and your hands are aligned with the bottom rail. The rails of the railroad track point in the direction of your target, e.g., the area where you want your drive to land on the fairway.

You can practice a one-piece takeaway by taking a short backswing. Bring the driver head back only to the 3 o'clock position and keep your left and right arms straight until you reach the 3 o'clock position with your arms.

Your hands and clubhead should travel parallel on the tracks as you take your clubhead to the 3 o'clock position.

Repeat this takeaway until it feels comfortable.

Then do several full swings.

Keep in mind you shouldn't try to swing harder. Instead, you are focusing on making good contact with the ball.

Keep hitting balls to grove this one-piece takeaway on a wide arc. You should see increased distance on your drives.

You Don't Have to Use Driver Off the Tee

The rules of golf allow you to use any club in your bag off the tee. Jack Nicklaus used his three-wood off the tee more often than he used his driver. And, Jimmy Demaret said, "You know what they say about big hitters...the woods are full of them."

Senior golfers may be hitting the green routinely in three shots on long par 4s. A shorter drive will make your third shot longer than what you are used to, but using a three metal or other lesser club on your drive will make you score better if you have difficulty in hitting a narrow fairway.

And, of course, it's better to make the green on a long par 4 in three shots compared to spending time looking for a lost ball in the rough, and then having to play your provisional.

Moreover, if there are undulating areas you would most likely hit to using your driver, it's better to hit a lesser club shorter to a flat area where your second shot is easier to hit off level ground.

Tee the ball up about a ¼ inch off the ground if you're using a long iron or hybrid instead of driver. And, as you go up in clubs (say a 5 iron), tee the ball closer to the ground since you don't want to hit the ball toward the top of the iron blade which will cost you distance.

Make a nice wide takeaway with a long iron or a hybrid and focus on making a smooth swing.

How to Avoid a Slice Off the Tee

A slice is common among senior golfers and can be caused by several things: First, a slice is caused by a very weak grip - which is having your left hand turned far to the left so you're unable to see the knuckles on your left hand.

Or, a slice could be caused by having your toe line and shoulders aimed too far to the left of your target. In other words, your right foot is forward in your stance creating an open stance, and your club face is aligned straight ahead.

Or, a slice could be caused by aligning your club face too far to the right of where your toe line and shoulders are pointing.

Or, a slice can be caused by an outside to inside swing which creates a clockwise spin on the ball causing it to sharply curve to the right.

If you're hitting into a strong wind, the amount of curve will increase proportionately to the strength of the wind, i.e., the stronger the wind, the more it will curve.

The more you aim to the left with your toe line and shoulder line, and the more you aim the club face to the right of your toe line and shoulders, the more you will slice the ball to your right.

To stop the slice, check the alignment of your toe line, shoulder line and club face to ensure you don't have too open of a stance.

Check your grip, and if you are using a weak grip, try taking a neutral grip, or even a strong grip as if you are going to hit a draw off the tee.

If you still don't know what is causing you to slice the ball, have a golf professional check if you are swinging from the outside to the inside. If you are, you may have to learn a new swing to get rid of the slice.

If you want to hit a severe slice intentionally, use a weak grip, put your right foot forward in your stance to create an open stance, have your toes and shoulders lined up way to the left of your target, and your club face lined up to the right of your target.

Or, if you want to severely hook the ball intentionally, do the opposite - use a very strong grip, and align your club face to the right of your target. Then drop your right foot far back so your toe line and shoulder are lined up even further to the right of your target than the clubface.

The more you aim to the right of your target with your toe and shoulder line, and the more you close your clubface, the more you will to hook the ball.

Turn Your Right Foot Out

Another way to make it easier for a senior golfer to drive the ball is to turn your right foot out which makes your hips open up more.

In a normal golf stance, your left foot is turned out anywhere from a 30 degree to a 45-degree angle to your torso, and your right foot is usually perpendicular (90 degrees) to your torso. When you take a normal stance with your right foot at a 90-degree angle with your shoulders, notice that your hips are square to your shoulders.

Now, turn your right foot out pointing your right toe toward the right – about a 110 to 120-degree angle with your shoulders. Notice that your hips are more open now, which allows you to make an easier turn when you draw the club back in one piece.

Turning your right foot out also helps keep you from swaying sideways when you swing at the ball. It forces you to rotate and turn the upper torso of your body instead of swaying sideways.

Take a Wider Stance

To Get More Distance, Take a Wider Stance. When you take a wider stance, you create a bigger arc. The larger the arc in your swing, the more clubhead speed you will generate.

Shoulder and Hip Turn

If you watch young players on the PGA Tour hit a drive in slow motion, you will see they rotate their upper body in a turning and twisting motion, so their shoulders turn past 90 degrees to where the ball is teed up. In fact, most of the young long-hitting PGA Tour Players turn their shoulders about 120 degrees, so their left shoulder is roughly 30 degrees behind the ball when they rotate their upper body.

Most golfers over 50 cannot physically turn their shoulders more than about 90 degrees.

Nevertheless, you can have one swing thought of turning your shoulders more (in a smooth and easy manner) when you want to hit a long drive. This one swing thought of trying to turn your shoulders more in an easy and relaxed manner will usually create more distance when driving the ball. Don't try to swing hard and concentrate on turning more than swinging hard as the more you turn, the faster the clubhead will go without you even consciously trying to swing faster.

The second part of hitting a longer drive is your hip turn. Most of the young long hitting PGA Tour Players turn their hips about 45 degrees while they simultaneously turn their shoulders 120 degrees. This creates a tight coil at the top of their swing - which results in a lot of clubhead speed on the downswing. This "coiling" results in long drives.

Golfers over 50 usually are able to turn their hips 45 degrees, especially if you raise your left heel up as you go into your backswing. You can also drop your right foot back in your stance, which makes it easier to rotate your hips more than you normally turn your hips.

Having one combined swing thought of making a good shoulder turn of 90 degrees, and a resulting hip turn of 45 degrees, you will automatically create a coiling at the top of your swing, and this will add distance to your drives.

Practice creating a tight coil turning your shoulders 90 degrees and your hips 45 degrees at the driving range. You shouldn't try to swing any harder. Relax as you try this with a steady and smooth tempo.

Turn Your Left Toe Out

Another way to create more clubhead speed is to turn your left toe out more when you take your stance. This will allow you to finish your swing easier, so your chest will finish turning after you strike the ball.

Iron Play – How to Have More Consistency.

There are many factors which cause you to strike the ball well one day, and then lose it on the next round, or even lose it on the next hole.

Basically, if you have a sound golf swing, you are going to be more consistent striking the ball even on bad days.

Golfers over 50 tend to have a variety of swings (modified by age over the years), and our first suggestion to increase consistency is to take a lesson with a PGA Teaching Pro and have him (or her) look at your golf swing with consistency in mind. See if the pro can recommend one or two things to modify your golf swing to help you strike the ball more consistently.

For example, one of our team took a lesson and the pro simply told him he was playing the ball in the wrong position when he took his stance. Our team member happened to be playing the ball slightly forward of where he should play the ball (depending on the club he was using). The pro made a slight adjustment moving the ball just a few millimeters (i.e. ¼ inch) back in his stance, and he is hitting the ball cleaner with a lot more consistency.

There are some things you may want to try on your own before taking a lesson with a pro.

1. Having the right stance is important for consistency. As you age, your back becomes more rounded, and instead of having a golf stance with a

straight back (which makes it easier to turn your upper body), you begin swaying sideways, or reaching down to strike the ball which causes unexpected mishits. Have a swing thought of standing tall and keeping your back straight with a slight bend forward. Allow your arms to be perpendicular to the ground, so they hang relaxed and down to the ground. Keep your knees slightly bent and stick your buttocks out which makes it easier to turn your upper body.

2. Legs moving too much? To keep your legs from moving too much, concentrate on making a good turn with your upper torso.

3. Eye-hand coordination deteriorates with age.[22] So, don't be too hard on yourself if you're not as consistent as you used to be in your younger years.

4. Varying degrees of flexibility cause inconsistent shots since flexibility also decreases with age.[23] Make sure you loosen up before playing and establish a routine daily stretching program for yourself like the stretching program suggested in Chapter 10 of this book.

Golf Swing Speed

As a person ages, golf swing speeds slow down. Generally, you can't swing as fast as you could when you were younger. Acceptance of that fact is important, so you don't wind up overswinging trying to physically force the ball to travel farther.

As you age, it's more important to concentrate on swinging smoothly and making good contact with the ball. Accept the fact you won't hit it as far as you could in your younger years, and it will make you have fewer errant shots and score better.

Swaying Laterally

If you find yourself swaying back and forth laterally instead of rotating your upper torso, turn your lead foot (left foot for right handed golfers) out at a 45-degree angle from your shoulder line. Having your left foot turned out will make it easier for you to avoid swaying side to side during your golf swing.

Swaying, instead of rotating, causes you to top the ball. Swaying also occurs when you don't start your golf swing by initiating the turn with your left side. This is because a golfer who sways, tends to move backward with his right side first.

Beginning your turn with your left shoulder will cause you to twist back automatically rather than sway back and forth laterally. It will help you turn your left side out of the way, so your right side will rotate and not sway back.

Also, turning your left foot out 45 degrees will help you to properly follow through with the shot after the club strikes the ball.

Shorten Your Backswing

As a person ages, the less coordination he will have.[24] A full backswing requires coordination.

If you take a full swing with your iron, sometimes you find your hands are not leading the club head. As you may know, your hands should be ahead of the iron club face, so you will be hitting down at the ball causing it to rise in the air and taking a divot.

It is easier if you are over 50 to take less of a backswing to increase the probability of having your hands lead the club face. Instead of taking a full swing with an iron, practice taking a three-quarter swing, or even a half swing, and you should see a difference in making more good contact with the ball.

Lowering the Kickpoint

The kickpoint in the shaft is the part of the shaft that is most flexible and has the most bend in it. The kickpoint affects the trajectory of the ball after you hit it. The lower the kickpoint is on your shaft, the higher the trajectory will be after you hit it.

The older we get, the harder it is to hit the ball on a high trajectory. There is a tendency to try and lift the ball into the air. If you try out an iron with a low kickpoint, you will hit the ball on a higher trajectory.

The Short Game

Senior golfers are usually above average in the short game area. But sometimes things go wrong such as chunking a pitch.

As explained before, as we age there is reduced coordination. If you are 50 yards out from the green and want to hit a delicate pitch close to the pin, you may wind up chunking the shot by thinking too much and trying to be too delicate.

It's embarrassing, especially when the other players are already on or just off the green, waiting for you to hit a second pitch after you've just chunked it on your first try.

Chunking a pitch is usually caused by slowing down the club just as you try to strike the ball. The slowing down of the downswing is usually due to trying too hard to be too precise with the shot.

To avoid this, take a narrow stance with your weight on your left side (for right handed golfers), and make a normal, relaxed pitch that automatically accelerates the club head on the downswing. If you take a shorter and relaxed backswing, there is less chance you will chunk the ball.

Distance in chipping is also controlled by how much of a backswing you take before striking the ball. Practice taking the club back half way (i.e. to the 9 o'clock position) and see how far the ball goes.

Then do another chip from the same spot but take it back only to the eight-thirty o'clock position, and so on down to the 7 o'clock position. This will get you used to the distance the ball will travel with a shortened backswing.

Also, practice shortening your backswing with different irons to get a feel for the distance with each club and with a shorter backswing.

90

Practice chipping as well with shorter backswings. A chip is a shot when you are on the fringe or close to the green and you use an iron as you would a putter brushing the ball off the ground.

Again, you don't want to deaccelerate on the downward swing which will cause a chunk and a mishit chip.

Take a narrow stance and keep your wrists locked with the back of your left hand pointed at the target. Play the ball back in your stance and take the club back a short way, keeping your wrists straight. And, keep your right bicep close to your right side so you won't be using too much of your arms. Relax and gently accelerate down when you strike the ball.

Think "Tick" when you take the club back and think "Tock" when you strike the ball, to create a good tempo when you chip the ball.

A pitch shot is usually played when you're within 60 yards of the green when you want to hit the ball high and land it softly on the green.

In pitching, as well as in chipping, you first select your landing area, and visualize a three-foot circle around the spot where you want the ball to land and focus on hitting the ball to that exact area.

Your landing area determines whether you are going to hit a high pitch, a medium height pitch or a low pitch. If you want to hit it high (so the ball will roll less on the green), play the ball forward in your stance.

If you want to hit it low and have the ball run more when it hits the green, play the ball further back in your stance with your hands in front of the ball.

One way to distinguish between a pitch shot and a chip shot, is a pitch shot spends the same - or more - time in the air and less time on the ground rolling.

The chip shot is the opposite and spends more time rolling.

A pitch is made using a pitching wedge using your normal stance. Hold the club loosely so it will easily slide under the ball.

As you get closer to the green, you narrow your stance more, and adjust the distance you want the ball to travel by limiting the amount of backswing you take before striking the ball.

That is, for shorter distances, you may only want to make a three quarter or half of a backswing before pitching the ball.

More about Chipping

Chipping is a shot used when you are a few feet off the green when you want the ball to travel only a short distance in the air, and land on the green and roll most of the distance on the green toward the pin.

You can use various clubs, but mostly irons or wedges, depending on how much distance you have between your ball and the landing area on the green. The less lofted the club, the more distance the ball will roll on the green.

After you selected your landing area and the appropriate club to chip with, take several short practice swings brushing the grass and feeling the texture of the grass with the clubhead.

Keep your wrists straight, and swing with your arms in line with your target. Put the ball back in your stance with your hands ahead since you want to keep the ball low, and land on your landing area and roll the rest of the way to the pin.

Place more weight on your left side. Take a slightly open stance so your arms can swing in line with your target.

Again, keep your left wrist straight and use a relaxed smooth short stroke. Focus on making good contact with the back of the ball.

Fringe Shots

If your ball is off the green on the fringe, consider keeping things simple and use your "Texas Wedge" aka your putter, to putt the ball over the fringe and onto the green to the pin.

You could chip it, but using your putter is simple, and might be easier if the fringe is smooth.

You hit the ball as you would a putt, but only hit it a little harder to get the ball through the longer grass on the fringe, and to roll freely to the pin once it reaches the green.

Three-metal off the collar. If your ball comes to rest on the fringe with high blades of grass directly behind the back of the ball, consider using your three-metal, five-metal, or hybrid to sweep at the grass and back of the ball using a putting stroke.

Choke down on the shaft to increase your chances of making good contact with the grass and back of the ball.

These clubs usually get through the long grass a lot easier and increase your percentages in hitting it closer to the pin.

Hybrid Chip

While most golfers use an iron if you have ten or more feet of fringe to get through plus a lot of green to work with, you might want to consider chipping with a hybrid instead of a wedge.

Choke down on the hybrid and play the ball back in your stance to increase your chances of making good contact with the ball.

The loft of the hybrid will get the ball briefly up in the air and bouncing low and rolling over the fringe and onto the green toward the pin.

Hitting balls off the fringe and onto the green with these clubs takes concentration and feel.

Like most anything, practicing shots around the green will make you better at using these as well as all the greenside shots.

If too much concentration over these shots gets to you, keep in mind, golf is a sport to be enjoyed. Relax, and don't be afraid to laugh.

Chipping from Downhill or Uphill Slopes

Your ball comes to rest on a steep downhill slope just off the green and you want to chip it. You pick your landing spot and visualize a one to two-foot circle around your landing spot.

It's best not to try and chip the ball up in the air (since the ground is already going downhill, the ball will roll quite a bit if it lands on a downslope). So, visualize chipping it on a lower trajectory.

Take a wide stance so you'll be better able to keep your balance, especially on a very steep downhill slope.

Angle your shoulders to match the contour of the slope. Again, a way to check if your shoulders match the downhill slope is to see if you can reach your left kneecap with your left hand.

Your practice swings need to brush the grass without stubbing the club into the ground and swing smoothly parallel with the slope of the hill.

Take note of where the club brushes the grass and address the ball in your stance at that point.

Hit the shot and follow through chipping the ball to your landing area.

Tiger Woods usually uses a sand wedge to chip with to put a reverse spin on the ball which keeps it from rolling too fast, and further away from the hole on a downhill chip.

For an uphill slope, you can use these same techniques but when doing your practice swings, note where the club brushes the upsloping ground and address the ball accordingly to avoid stubbing your club into the ground.

The uphill slope will add more loft to your club to make the chip go higher in the air, so you need to make an adjustment for this when you select your landing area.

Pitching Over a Greenside Sand Bunker

If you must pitch over a greenside bunker, some players call this, "The Easiest Shot in Golf." They are actually telling you it's extremely easy to pitch it right into the bunker. By the way, the second easiest shot in golf is leaving it in the bunker when you try to hit it out of the sand bunker you just flubbed your pitch into.

It's feels intimidating at times to chip from a tight lie over a deep trap. But, there is an easy method. Play the ball back in your stance using a high lofted club. Your hands should be in front of the ball, and most of your weight is forward on your left side. This set-up helps you strike the ball first and not flub it into the bunker.

Grip the club lightly so the clubhead will slide under the ball more easily. Keep your wrists straight, and take an easy, relaxed half swing. Allow the loft of the club to raise the ball over the bunker, onto the green and rolling toward the pin.

By the way, Tom Watson said his easiest shot in golf was a shot he learned from Ray Floyd - chipping with a putting stroke.

The Drop Shot

A drop shot is used when your ball is in deep, heavy grass a foot or more high very near or around the green.

If you were further away from the green in heavy grass you most likely would use a lot of force and hit the ball out of the heavy grass.

A drop shot is used when you want to get the ball just slightly out of the heavy grass and rolling on the green. It is a very delicate shot you need to practice.

Since the grass is thick and heavy, if you tried to make a full smooth swing at the ball, you risk stubbing the shot, with the heavy grass getting gnarled around and catching the club head, leaving the ball in the deep grass.

If you took a full powerful swing at the ball, you risk fully catching the ball and hitting it too far.

To do a drop shot, or what is sometimes called a "pop-out" shot, take a high lofted club like a 60-degree wedge and chop down quickly at the back of the ball with it. You need to accelerate the club downward at a steep angle directly behind the ball.

The ball should pop out on to the green and roll toward your target with little or no spin on the ball.

Here is a simple drill: Put 10 balls near the edge of the practice green in deep, thick grass. Chop down on the back of the ball popping it out and rolling on the green. See how close you can get it to the pin.

Put 10 balls in the same heavy rough but try to force the ball out by taking a full smooth swing or a forceful swing and compare your results to popping the ball out doing a drop shot.

The Bump and Run Shot

There's an old saying, "Your worst pitch isn't going to be better than your worst chip," and, there is a lesser known saying, "You don't have to hit the ball gracefully into the air, if you don't have to, since there's no pictures on scorecards."

A bump and run shot is a low pitch shot used about 40 yards or less to the green.

Use a bump and run shot when there is a clear path to the pin without any obstacles or hazards in your way.

Take a narrow stance, play the ball back in your stance with your hands slightly ahead.

You hit the shot with an iron of your choice planning to carry the ball halfway in the air on a low trajectory to the pin and allowing the ball to run on the ground the other halfway to the pin.

If the green is small and you have a clear path to the pin, it's easier to judge the distance by running the ball up on a low trajectory in this manner than to hit it high in the air and have the ball possibly roll off the side or back of the green.

A bump and run shot is not a glamourous shot, but if it gets the job done and if you feel relaxed about using a bump and run shot, then go for it and use it more often when the opportunity is there.

Hitting into the Bank Shot.

The hit it into the bank shot is a shot played when your ball is close to the green, and there is a bank or a berm you must hit the ball over to get the ball on the green close to the pin, and you don't want the ball to go too far past.

If there isn't much green to work with, chances are if you chip it up in the air over the berm and land it on the green, the ball will roll further away from the pin than you are already.

You could try a flop shot instead of the bank shot. The bank shot is an alternative to a flop shot. Choose whichever shot you have the most confidence in.

To do a bank shot, pitch the ball directly into the face of the bank. When the ball hits the face of the bank, it will slow the speed of the ball down, and the ball will pop up in the air and slowly roll onto the green near the pin.

Play the ball back in your stance and use a narrow stance with your hands ahead of the ball.

Hitting a ball into a bank takes practice to get a good feel for this shot and few golfers ever practice it. If the practice area has a chipping green with a bank, drop ten practice balls and hit them into the side of the bank trying to stop the ball within 10 feet from where the green begins, i.e. imagine you only have about 10 feet of green to work with.

Try using different irons and see how many balls you keep within 10 feet.

Sand Shots

When you take your stance in the bunker, bend your knees more as your legs and feet need to be steady so you won't slip in the sand.

Put most of your weight on your left side which will stop you from falling back when you strike the sand.

For greenside bunkers, your goal is to have your clubhead enter the sand behind the ball and allow the sand to lift the ball out toward your target.

Play the ball slightly ahead of the middle of your upper body since you want your club to enter the sand behind the ball. Or, focus on a spot in the sand like a pebble an inch or half-inch behind the ball. Determine how much sand you will take – the more sand you take (say an inch behind the ball) the less the ball will travel, and vice-versa.

Be confident before you start your swing in your choice of the spot in the sand you want the edge of your sand wedge to enter behind the ball, so you won't be hesitating or slowing the club on your downswing.

Make a smooth swing using your arms only. Practicing sand shots more will give you added confidence, of course. Some teaching pros, after having the student execute the proper technique, will have the student take a bucket of balls and hit nothing but sand shots for an hour. After that hour period, hitting a ball out of the sand becomes routine.

For a normal bunker shot, use a sand wedge and put most of your weight on your left side.

The sand wedge clubface should be open. Since you are opening the club face, aim to the left of your target.

Hit one to two inches behind the ball instead of hitting the ball directly. Your clubhead enters the sand and lifts the sand and the ball out of the trap in one swing.

Be sure to follow through with your shot. Swing smoothly and complete your swing.

Occasionally, recreational golfers stop their swing once they feel the sand wedge enter the sand behind the ball, but finishing your swing is important to get the ball out of the sand. Finish your shot with your body facing your target.

Buried "Fried Egg" Bunker Shot

If your ball is buried in the bunker, close your club face, and aim it directly at the target.

A large amount of sand or damp sand will give a larger amount of resistance to your club head, so you must use a lot more force in your swing.

Swing on a steep angle down at the ball since your club head is going to dig a larger amount of sand out with the ball.

Wet Sand Bunker Shots

Heavy wet sand offers a lot more resistance, and it's very difficult to dig a sand wedge into heavy wet sand to get the ball out.

Consider using a high lofted club like a lob wedge, to skim the ball off the top of the wet sand and out of the bunker.

It's easier to skim the ball with a lob wedge off the top of wet sand and hit the ball off the sand as if you are doing a flop shot. Open the club face and choke down on the lob wedge. Then skim the ball off the wet sand with a lob wedge hitting roughly a half-inch or less behind the ball.

Wet sand is a problem for a senior golfer since it's difficult for an older golfer to dig into heavy wet sand of a greenside bunker. Instead of trying to dig the ball out of wet sand with a sand wedge, first determine if you can use your putter or other iron or a utility club to putt the ball over the wet sand onto the green.

If there is a lip on the greenside bunker preventing this, use the lob wedge and do a flop shot swing to skim the ball off the top of the sand onto the green.

Flop Shots

Flop shots are made with a lob wedge – usually having 60-64 degrees of loft.

Open the face of your lob wedge behind the ball, so the backside of the wedge is almost touching the top of the wet sand.

Keep your weight forward in your stance and focus on accelerating your swing smoothly to slip the club under the ball. Keep a loose grip to allow the club head to slide under the ball. Keep your left arm straight and remember not to break your wrists as you swing down at the ball resting on top of the wet sand.

Take the club back in one piece - without breaking your wrists. Allow the clubhead to slip under the ball and pop it into the air as you accelerate the club on the downswing slipping the club face under the ball. The faster you swing, the higher the ball will rise.

If the ball is plugged in wet sand, you don't have much choice other than digging it out with a heavier swing than normal.

If the sand is dry and light (which your club can easily pass through), focus on the hosel entering the sand next to the ball. Pick a spot on the sand behind the ball but next to it to focus on. Swing the hosel through the sand as if there were no clubface attached to it. This helps you swing with an accelerating downward swing and make a good follow through.

Putting

It's been shown putting ability decreases with age. On average, the ability to putt well starts in the early

30s then dramatically decreases as you near 50 years of age.[25]

When you take your stance, position your head so your eyes are directly over the ball. When your eyes are directly over the ball, it is easier for you to swing the putter back and forth in a straight line.

Keep your head still and down looking at the ball before and after you stroke the putt. Raising your head immediately after you strike the ball will likely cause the putt to go off line.

Jordan Spieth has gone on record by recommending keeping the back of your left hand moving toward the target with your wrists firm. Your wrists should stay firm through the putting stroke and the only movement you should have is with your shoulders. Using your wrists will cause the putt to go off line more than if you kept your wrists firm.

Peter Senior is a well-known 58-year-old Australian professional golfer who is famous for his excellent putting ability. He practices on the putting green by first hitting putts no longer than 10 feet to get the feel of the speed of the green.

After he is done with that and assuming there is room on the practice green, he picks a hole on the putting green that is farthest away from him to practice two putting very long putts. He tries to two-putt at least 20 long putts without having a three putt. Peter said, "The reason people three-putt is they make a bad first putt which is the most important putt when you're very far from the hole."

DRILL:

Try putting for a few minutes doing putts 10 feet or less to get a feel for the speed of the practice green. After that, stand at one end of the practice green, and try to make at least 5 (or more if you like) two-putts to the furthest hole away from you.

You can even compete with another putter to see who can make the most two putts out of say 10 balls, to a hole very far away from both of you on the practice green.

6. GOLF EQUIPMENT AND ACCESSORIES

Your old set of golf clubs may not be the best suited for you as the years go by. Current technology such as radar allows a professional golf instructor to fit you with the right clubs and club shafts with the right flexibility and kickpoint to match your swing for maximum distance, good ball striking, and consistency. Driver loft can also be tested and golfers with lower swing speed may hit it farther using a driver with a 12.5-degree loft.

People come in all shapes and sizes. As people age, their swing speed and weight of clubs are more of a factor. Hybrids make it easier to get a golf ball in the air because of the engineering behind a hybrid which has a protruding bottom edge on the head of the club slightly ahead of the shaft and hosel.

All Hybrid Set

A hybrid is an easy club for seniors to hit. There are golf sets available with hybrids substituting for irons. We don't recommend an all hybrid set since we like the feel of the higher irons. But it is an individual decision for you to make. There are complete hybrid sets available at your local golf retail shop.

Hybrids are similar to fairway woods and are more forgiving than long irons. They are smaller than fairway woods but easier to hit and more forgiving.

Hybrids are explained in detail in our book, "Golf Tips and Adult Golf Jokes." Here is an excerpt:

"A hybrid or a rescue club can take the place of a 2, 3, 4, or 5-iron. Hybrids shafts are shorter than fairway woods, but longer than the shafts of irons.

"A hybrid with a 17 degree to 19-degree loft is equal to a two iron.

"A hybrid with a 19-degree to 21-degree loft is equal to a three iron.

"A hybrid with a 22 to 23-degree loft is equal to a 4 iron.

"And, a hybrid with a 24 to 27-degree loft is equal to a 5 iron.

"You should play the ball in your stance similar to where you play the ball using the equivalent iron.

"You strike the ball on your downward swing just as you do with your irons.

"Irons have leading edges in a direct even line with the shaft and hosel, but hybrids have a leading edge which protrudes out from the shaft and hosel making it easier to hit the ball into the air.

"You swing with a hybrid as you would an iron and strike the ball on the downswing of your swing arc, compressing the ball with your clubhead. You want to hit the ball an instant before the club head strikes the ground while still on the downward part of your swing arc.

"You play the ball between the middle of your stance and your left heel. Keep in mind the hybrid has a longer shaft than an iron, so you play it forward of the center of your stance."

"Play the ball a bit further back than if you were using a five-metal since you want the clubhead to strike the ball an instant before it bottoms out at the bottom of your swing arc."

Visit your golf retailer if you are interested in having more hybrids in your bag and make your own personal decision. Some golfers swear by them and play several shots better.

Radar Will Give You the Right Clubs

Keep in mind, with all the products and brands on the market today, the best way to find golf clubs that will suit you is to be tested under a radar device and golf simulator.

For example, if you are being tested for a new Driver, the golf club consultant should change the loft of the driver club face, the shafts trying different shafts with varying flexibility, kick points, lengths, etc. and compare the results to see what best works.

Based on the distances you hit each club, you may decide to forego getting a three-metal, and just stick with a five-metal which is generally an easier club to hit because of its shorter shaft, and especially if you get about the same distance with it as you would with a three-metal. It should take at least an hour of testing to find what's best for you.

The equipment on the market today is complicated. In our opinion, TaylorMade has an amazing M1 Driver (which is not very forgiving for the average golfer), and TaylorMade's M2 Driver is well suited for the average player.

Callaway has come out with an Epic driver designed with the assistance of Boeing engineers who helped design a club head that easily moves through the air. Titleist, Ping, and others have excellent drivers. It all comes down to what suits you best.

Putters, putter weights, length of putter shafts, and thicker putter grips are very personal to each golfer. A putter that works well for one person, may not work for you. It may take you time to find the right putter which feels most comfortable and consistent with your putting style. If you can afford it, a Scotty Cameron putter is an excellent choice. Seniors seem to favor mallet head putters as discussed further in this Chapter since it has more alignment lines than a blade putter.

Most all well-known golf retailers have the right test equipment to select the right clubs for you, and have professional staff that will recommend the right clubs, and grips (remember to try out arthritic grips, or thicker grips too).

Golf Balls

Jack Nicklaus has 3 golf balls[26] he recommends, and one of them is specifically for seniors or anyone with a low swing speed. Bridgestone makes these golf balls.[27]

Some other information on golf balls designed for low swing speeds and for more control are:

Callaway Supersoft Golf Ball

Srixon AD333 Golf Balls

TaylorMade Tour Preferred Golf Balls

Titleist DT Solo Golf Balls

These golf balls have excellent feel and may (or may not help your game), and you need to try them out and make your own decision.

Golf Gloves

Bionic Golf Gloves have gloves specially made for senior golfers. www.bionicgloves.com This company makes a special relief grip for golfers who suffer from arthritis which make it easier to grip the club. Their website has a special tab for "Arthritis".

Aids to Assist Bad Backs

The UprightGolf Company has items that will assist senior golfers from bending over to tee up balls, etc. www.uprightgolf.com. They have devices to assist picking up balls from the hole, marking your ball on the green, etc.

Golf Carts for Disabled Golfers

The SoloRider golf cart company makes golf carts for disabled golfers for senior golfers or any golfer who has difficulty walking. www.solorider.com.

Putters

Regardless of your age, choosing a putter is a personal decision and we don't recommend one putter over another since each golfer needs to choose a putter which feels right and produces the best results.

There are generally two types of putters: Mallet head putters and blade putters. Mallet head putters have a large head and more alignment markings than blade putters. Some say mallet head putters are better for senior golfers since the alignment markings are larger and easier to see. Most golf retail shops have practice areas where you can see which putter suits you best.

The correct choice of a putter depends on your putting stroke – i.e., whether you have a straight back and through motion (mallet head putters are good for this type of putting stroke), or a have a curved motion putting stroke (blade putters would suit you better for a curved stroke). Have a golf professional look at your putting stroke and give you a recommendation on what type of putter to use.

7. DIET SUGGESTIONS

Bernhard Langer revealed a lot about his diet and keeping fit. He said, "I think one of the keys is to keep the metabolism going."

"You need to eat constantly, *not large portions* but you need to eat while playing, and a lot of people don't seem to agree with that."

Bernhard eats bananas, nuts, and other fruits on the course. He snacks to prevent his blood sugar getting low which makes him a little fatigued and he doesn't focus as well as he can when he snacks.

Tiger Woods, and many other excellent and fit players have a simple diet with an egg-white omelet and vegetables for breakfast. Lean meats, seafood, fruits, and vegetables for other meals and they avoid junk food, cheeseburgers, fries, etc.

They eat high protein and low-fat lunches, and dinners such as grilled chicken, a salad, fish, and vegetables. Diets are very important since no matter how hard you train, your diet may be an obstacle to your golf fitness.

What and how much you eat depends on your physique. People have different shapes, sizes, etc., and the number of calories required each day varies in accordance with your age, bone structure, height, and metabolism. Delicious foods are unfortunately around everywhere you go, and hard to avoid at times.

Most doctors recommend consulting with your personal physician to set realistic goals if you're seeking weight loss as well as a good diet. Setting small goals and reaching those goals gives you a positive feeling of success which motivates you to follow the diet.

If you study the diets of what well known winning golfers eat, you gain insight into healthy eating habits for golfers.

For example, Jordan Spieth has revealed he eats a vegetable omelet with baked sweet potato for breakfast.

For lunch, he'll eat lean fish, more vegetables, brown rice, and lentils. And for dinner, he'll eat a protein like red meat with more vegetables, quinoa, and for snacks on the course, he likes granola. Of course, Jordan is a long way from being 50 plus years old, but we gain insight from what he eats to perform well on the course.

The Basic Logical Rule for Losing Weight

If you want to get yourself trim and stronger, read the logic on diets as explained by Michael Matthews in his bestselling book, "Bigger, Leaner Stronger."

Mr. Matthews points out, "When you give your body more calories than it burns off, it stores fat."

And, "When you give your body less calories than it burns throughout the day, it must make up for that deficit by burning its own energy stores (fat), which leads to fat loss."

It's not complicated. He explains no matter what kinds of food a person eats in his diet, if you store more calories than you use, you won't lose weight.

Of course, being overweight makes you less flexible. If you are overweight, and can't seem to lose weight, you are simply taking in more calories than you expend during the day.

We all know it's good to avoid saturated fats since it's very unhealthy. Processed foods like breads, pancakes, bagels, crackers, pretzels, etc. have lots of calories - meaning it's difficult to lose weight if you eat these foods.

Other foods to avoid (or seldom eat) which will make it easier for your body to lose weight, are soft drinks with a lot of sugar, fruit juices, pies, cakes, cookies, sugar sweetened candies, ice cream, etc.

Also, it's best to avoid fatty foods such as butter, cheese, mayonnaise, etc. and substitute healthy fats olive oil, avocados, walnuts, salmon, etc.

Each person has their own lifestyle. Some lead active lifestyles and expend a lot of energy, while others lead sedentary lifestyles spending less energy. Adjust the amount of food in your daily life to make sure you don't take in more calories than you expend.

One simple helpful way is not to eat anything late in the evening, or say, nothing after 6:30 pm every evening.

Overall, it's basically two things that will lower your weight and you need to do these together: Diet and Exercise. And, the essential point is to eat less calories than your body expends daily, and to eat natural foods and avoid processed foods and have an exercise program to burn calories. That objective will keep you trim and give your body a good look.

Eating before a golf round.

It is best not to eat a meal right before playing golf. Your digestive system needs blood to digest which means your brain and muscles will have less which will affect your concentration and golfing skills.

It's best to eat a meal an hour and a half before you begin our golf round. Complex carbohydrates are good to eat since they will give you a slow energy release and help your mental concentration and muscular system.

Drink plenty of water to make sure you're hydrated. When you become dehydrated during a hot weather golf round, you may become faint, and could even pass out in case of severe dehydration.

Alcohol increases dehydration, and if you are perspiring in addition to drinking alcohol during a hot afternoon of golf, you won't be playing up to your capability.

Drink a glass of water before you start playing on a warm day and take your water bottle with you.

What to Eat While Playing Golf

You want to maintain a normal blood sugar level during your round so fresh fruit such as bananas, apples, dried fruit are helpful to you, as well as nuts like walnuts, pumpkin seeds, and other nuts.

Eat only small amounts so you won't lose concentration, since the more you eat during a golf round, the more blood will be diverted from your brain. Drink or sip water during the round as well.

What To Eat After A Round Of Golf

Most of us enjoy a refreshing ice-cold beer, or another alcoholic beverage after the round, especially on warm days. The American Heart Association recommends alcohol in moderation which means two drinks of alcohol a day for men and one drink per day for women. Having a side glass of water is a good idea too whenever you drink alcoholic beverages.

After a round, it's good to eat a small amount of protein (e.g., grilled chicken) and carbohydrate-rich foods (e.g., nuts, berries) to replenish your blood sugar level.

Diets for athletic seniors

The number of seniors who engage in regular athletic activity is increasing. This is because it is becoming more well-known that a regular exercises program vs. exercising now and then, will offset or delay the negative effects of ageing.

A regular exercise program will also increase your psychological well-being.

Many scientific studies have been done which have found seniors who regularly exercise and eat a healthy diet are in better shape than people many years younger who don't regularly exercise or have a healthy diet.[28]

The American Heart Association recommends you should eat fruits and vegetables, whole grains, skinless poultry, and fish and other natural foods.[29]

As you age, it's best to avoid saturated fats, trans fats, salt, sweets, and drinks with a high sugar content.[30]

If you choose to eat red meats, choose lean red meats like venison, bison, or even Ostrich (ostrich is a lean red meat). It's better to eat fish rich in Omega-3s, such as halibut, herring, mackerel, oysters, salmon, sardines, trout, or tuna, as these are heart healthy according to the American Heart Association.

8. WAYS TO HAVE MORE FUN PLAYING GOLF

"Today's seniors aren't those of yesteryear."

"These are people who think they are 10 to 15 years younger, and act that way too."

"They still play golf but a lot of them scuba dive, too."

> *- Keith Vieira*

Use the Right Tees

There's a lot written about how older golfers can increase distance. But, there's no way as far as we know on escaping "Father Time". Age creeps in even though you maintain your body the best you can by exercising, a good diet, and a positive attitude.

Ideally, it's great to play golf where you can reach the green using an iron or a hybrid (rather than hitting driver and three-metal all day). Years ago, the PGA recommended a golfer should review the total yardage of the course and make the decision on what tees to play based on the average length of your drives:

The PGA recommended if you drive the ball an average distance of 275 yards, the total length of the course you should play is around 6700 to 6,900 yards.

If your average drive is 250 yards, the total length should play is 6,200 to 6,400 yards.

If your average drive is 225 yards, the total length you should play is 5800 - 6,000 yards.

And, if your average drive is around 200 yards, the total length should be 5200 – 5400 yards.

Generally, it's more fun being able to reach a green in regulation, so try playing the tees the PGA recommends for your average driving distance.

Most golf courses offer three sets of tees, Ladies', Mens' and Championship tees. However, it seems we are getting away from extremely long and difficult courses and there are a lot of golf courses around offering more sets of tees, since the current majority of golfers who play the game are over 50 years old.[31]

Exciting and Enjoyable Golf Formats

A $3 Nassau can get old. If you play with a regular foursome and throw balls up on the first tee box to determine partners, all four players usually know from experience who is going to prevail. So here are new golf formats you might want to enjoy.

Try playing "Snake" to improve your putting game. It's a simple fun game which is played on each green during a round and helps you avoid 3 putting and you will score better.

"Snake" goes like this: Starting with the first green, if you are the last person to three-putt on the green you are handed a rubber snake. If you are holding the snake as you walk off the 18th green, you lose whatever you originally wagered.

For example, say you are on the first green and you three-putt, you are given the "Snake", but if another player on the first green three putts after you, the snake passes to him.

128

You can pick up a rubber snake at a dollar shop. If you don't have one, you can use most anything (rubber frog, rubber chicken, etc.) as a substitute to pass along to a player who is the last one to three-putt on a green.

Remember, if two or more players three putt on the same green, then the last person to three-putt on the green gets the snake. So, consider putting out if you are sure you will make the putt to put more pressure on those that still have to putt (and be confident you can make it).

Before starting the round, agree on the amount the last person to hold the snake will owe each golfer after the 18th green.

If you don't want bet say, $10 a player, bet the loser buys a round of drinks for the rest. It's whatever you all decide.

If you want to add more tension to the Snake putting game, you can begin the betting at 25 cents, and agree the 25-cent amount is doubled each time the snake is passed during the round. Keep in mind, this can get expensive, of course, especially if you are playing a course with difficult greens.

If you all agree to start at 25 cents, and the snake is passed only 8 times, the person who walks off the 18th green owes $32 to each of the other 3 players or a total of $96.

Doubling the bet increases the pressure as the snake is passed on more (to say the least), especially as you approach the 18th green. Players with the snake have been known to layup, then pitch or chip the ball close to the pin to avoid having to deal with a long putt. We don't recommend large betting which may be over the legal limit depending on the local government laws that apply to you.

If you want to add some laughs, you can agree before the round to allow players to make any kind of snake sounds (Hisses…. or, rattles, etc.) while a player is trying not to three-putt. If you are playing with a rubber chicken, allow clucking sounds, etc.

In any event, this game will help you stop three-putting. It will make you think about your putting more and your overall scoring will improve.

"Low Putts" is another game which tends to lower your overall score. Before the round is started, 4 players put an agreed amount, say $10 each (or any agreed amount), into a "Low putts" pot.

During the round, you exchange scorecards, and you keep track of the other player's putts as well as your own putts. The golfer with the least number of putts over 18 holes wins the pot. Ties divide the pot accordingly.

This popular side game can also be used in golf tournaments, as the more people you have contributing to the "Low putts pot," the better.

"No Putts" is a game for good tee to green players. The game is based on other shots except putts. And, it's a great game to choose if the greens aren't in good shape and the players have approximately the same handicap.

Each player puts $10 (or any agreed amount) into a "No Putts" pot. You exchange scorecards and keep track of the player's putts (as well as your own putts) on each green throughout the round. At the end of the round, you reduce the total score of the round by the number of putts taken, and the result is the total shots made off the green.

The player with the lowest score of shots made off the green wins the pot.

If you want to improve your ability to choose a conservative safe shot, try "Trouble." Trouble is a game to help you strategize a golf round and is great for senior golfers. You want to avoid any trouble and play conservatively.

It does not matter what the total score of your golf round is, you can win this game even if you shoot 110 or worse, if you try not to hit your ball where it shouldn't go.

In other words, the player who gets into the least amount of trouble during the golf round wins the pot.

Before starting the round, players contribute $5 (or another agreed amount) into the pot. The player with the lowest number of points wins the pot (or divide it up anyway you decide with 1st, 2nd, or 3rd places).

During the round, points are assessed against a player for hitting his ball into trouble as follows:

Hitting into a bunker – 1 point.

Hitting into a water hazard or any marked hazard area – 2 points.

Hitting Out of Bounds – 3 points.

The player with the lowest amount of points (no matter what your golf score is) wins the pot and any ties proportionately divide the pot. Or, you can have a chip off to determine a winner.

The above version of Trouble is simple and straightforward. Another version of this game assesses points for other mistakes when playing "Trouble" such as three putting (1 point), or four putting (2 points), or topping/chunking/missing the ball (1 point).

Another game is our version of "Wolf for Seniors." "Wolf" is well known and very popular and has many versions and our favorite way to play Wolf goes like this:

Throw 4 balls up in the air to establish the order of teeing off by how close the balls come to rest to the person throwing the balls in the air. Player 1 being the closest, and so on.

If two balls land the same distance away, toss the four balls up again until there's a clear order.

Each player's number establishes the rotation for teeing off on the first 16 holes with these special rules:

The "Wolf" (Player 4 on the first hole) tees off last. The other players follow their number sequence in teeing off and use the same rotation order in teeing off over the first 16 holes.

Player 1 tees off first on the first hole, and Player 4 is automatically the "Wolf".

Player 2 tees off first on the second hole (and Player 1 is the last to tee off on the second hole and becomes the "Wolf").

Player 3 tees off first on the third hole (and Player 2 tees off last on the third hole and becomes the "Wolf" on the third hole).

Player 4 tees off first on the fourth hole (and Player 3 becomes the "Wolf" on the fourth hole).

And so on, with Player 1 teeing off first on the fifth hole (and Player 4 becomes the "Wolf" again on the fifth hole).

Before starting the round, the players agree on an amount each hole is worth (for example, assume you all agree on playing each hole for $1).

The player with the lowest score wins the amount the hole is worth (in our example, the lowest score wins $1 for the hole). If there is a tie for the lowest score, it's a wash, and the players go on to the next hole where another player (following in the set rotation) is the Wolf.

Since there are four players, and to give everyone four opportunities to be the Wolf, you only play the first 16 holes in this same rotation order for the first 16 holes.

Wolf gets interesting since the Wolf, who tees off last, watches the other players tee off. After each drive, the Wolf must decide if he wants the player who just hit his drive, as his partner on the hole.

In other words, being the Wolf gives you an advantage of electing to play with a good partner to help you win the hole for $1.

The Wolf, teeing off last, must choose a golfer right when he sees the golfer's tee shot. In other words, he can't wait until he sees all three drives and must choose right after seeing the drive. The Wolf can't watch three drives and then pick a partner – he can only pick a partner immediately after seeing the drive.

When the Wolf chooses a partner, then it's a two-man team vs. the other two-man team playing match play for that hole. Of course, a high handicapper usually chooses a better player if he sees the better player hit a good drive.

For example, if the Wolf's partner gets a four, and the other two players get a 5 and a 6, and you, as the Wolf get a 6. You and your chosen partner win $1 from the other two players on this hole because your partner had the lowest score on the hole which makes your team winners for that hole.

If the other team had a lower score than you and your chosen partner on the first hole, then the other team would have won $1 from you and your chosen player.

If there was a tie, no one would win anything, and you go to the next hole where another player has a turn at being the Wolf.

Before anyone tees off, whoever is the Wolf has an option to say to the other 3 players he is going to be a "Lone Wolf" on the hole. This option triples the bet (to $3 in our example).

He must call out that he will be the "Lone Wolf" before anyone tees off. If he wins the hole, he wins $3 from each player. If he doesn't beat the lowest score he owes $3 to each of the other players.

Wolf is played with full handicaps, so the scores are all net scores, of course.

If the Wolf doesn't take a partner after viewing the first three drives, the Wolf is deemed to be automatically playing the hole as the "Lone Wolf" but this type of "Lone Wolf" is only playing for double the bet for the hole (i.e. for $2 and the Wolf would win $2 from each player if he has the lowest score, or loses $2 to each player if any of the other three scores a net score lower).

When you get to the 17th tee, whoever is losing the most is automatically the "Wolf" for that hole to give him an opportunity to lessen his losses.

The same applies to the 18th tee whoever is in last place after finishing the 17th hole, becomes the Wolf on the 18th tee.

Playing Wolf builds confidence in your game. And, it also helps you learn to trust another person.

It's up to you, but we give a golfer with a handicap over 25, a "mulligan" every time it is his turn to be the Wolf. This helps his chances and decision making before anyone tees off.

"Bingo, Bango, Bongo" can be played between two, three and four players. This game is good for players with different handicaps. High handicappers can win over low handicappers, and short hitters can win over big hitters.

Before the round, the players contribute to a pot and usually the winner will take all. In the event of ties, the pot is divided evenly among them.

The player with the most Bingo Bango Bongo points wins. Points are earned during the round starting with the first hole in this manner:

The first player to get his ball on the green wins 1 point – the "Bingo Point."

The first player to get his ball closest to the pin after all balls are on the green wins 1 point – the "Bango point."

And, the first player to get his ball into the hole wins 1 point – the "Bongo point."

The points are added at the end of the round and the highest point total wins the pot.

Throughout the round, the etiquette rule of "The player who is away" must play first. This gives a shorter hitter a chance to be first on the green – and win the Bingo point.

Also, the high handicapper may be off the green, say just on the fringe, while the low handicapper may already be on the green. This gives the high handicapper a chance to earn the bango point by chipping closest to the pin.

Players follow customary "Honors" with the lowest score teeing off first. This gives a low handicapper who might have gotten the lowest score on the last hole before a par 3 hole, a chance to win the Bingo point if he tees first on a par 3.

There are variations. The above version is simple and basic Bingo, Bango Bongo but you can add a bonus point (or double points) if a player wins all three points on a single hole. It's whatever you all decide.

Our version of "Greensomes" are played with 2-man teams with all 4 players teeing off, selecting the best drive and playing alternating shots until the ball is holed out.

Another way of describing Greensomes is whoever hit the drive in your 2-man team, steps aside and the other member of the two-man team hits the next shot and then alternate shots until the ball is holed.

The competition is stroke play and in our version, we determine each team's handicap by adding 60% of the lower handicap to 40% of the higher handicap. We use that total for the 2-man team's handicap.

"Gruesomes" is a variation of Greensomes except instead of playing the best drive, the opposing team selects the worse drive and play continues with alternate shots in the same manner as Greensomes.

As a change of pace, the foursome you play in may want to play a Three Club Monte with a two-man scramble format. This game will improve your versatility as it gives you a chance to consider each shot with another golfer and discuss how best to do it with only a few clubs.

Each player chooses 3 clubs (such as a wedge, 5 Iron and a hybrid), and plays the round with those three clubs.

Another benefit of Three Club Monte is a refreshing break from the usual play and expanding your specialty shots and improvisation.

You play it with a partner against the other two in a foursome as a two-man scramble where you choose the best positioned drive, then both of you hit from where your best drive was. Then both of you hit the next shot and select the best one, and so on until the ball is holed out.

Balls are thrown up on the first tee and the two balls landing closest together are partners. Handicaps for the teams are determined by adding 60% of the low handicap to 40% of the high handicap and the total is the team handicap.

You can play match play for an agreed amount per hole. Or, you can all contribute equally to a Three Club Monte Scramble Pot, winning team takes all. Or, you can play for drinks, or bet any way you all agree on.

"MeToos and FUs." Generally, a "MeToo", is where you can move your shot to someone else's in your group on a hole, be it a drive, iron shot, chip, putt, i.e. any shot. You must declare a "MeToo" after seeing the shot and before hitting your next shot.

If you're playing against a single opponent, or an opposing team, you can call a "MeToo" only against your opponent, or the opposing team (as the case might be), and you place your ball where the other shot is and play your shot from there. In case your opponent sinks a putt or chips in, you can call a "MeToo" and consider your ball holed out.

If you're playing one player vs. one player, only the player who calls a "MeToo" can pick up and move his ball to the other shot he called a "MeToo" on.

If you're playing individual play in a foursome, all three of the other players can use a "MeToo" on another player's shot, such as a great drive or an iron shot.

If you're playing in two-man teams, both team members can move their balls to the opposing shot when the team calls a "MeToo" against one of the opposing team member's shot.

This game can become a refreshing dose of brainless fun if one of your adversaries makes a long putt or chip. After any putt is made, you put your ball in the hole after you call "MeToo" (or, in other words, simply pick up counting your own putt as holed out like the putt that just went in).

Before you start the round, you all must agree on the number of "MeToos" a player or team can use before starting the round.

Matches tend to be a lot more competitive.

Suggestion: Try playing one "MeToo" a side to start with and see how the round goes. Add more later if you all agree.

A "FU" (Forget You) is the opposite of a "MeToo." "FUs" are used when you hit into a bunker, a water hazard, O.B., etc.

A "FU" allows you to have your opponent (or the opposing team) place his (or both other team balls) ball within 6 inches of where your unfortunate ball landed including hazards, water, OB, etc. on a hole.

You can just play "MeToos" without allowing "FUs", and vice-versa, or, you can play both "MeToos" and "FUs" together.

A "MeToo" and "FU" cannot be declared on the same golf hole. If you declare "MeToo," your opponent(s) cannot declare "FU" on that hole, and vice versa.

143

Agree on the number of FUs before starting the round. Start with one FU a side.

Ways to Keep Positive During Delays and Tee Backups

The bad part of any delay is loss of rhythm. If you're having a good round, and then turn the corner to the next tee box and see two foursomes ahead of you waiting to tee off on a difficult par 3.

If there's nothing you can do to correct the situation, then relax. Relaxation is very important. Don't let your muscles tense up due to the aggravating situation. We like to trade jokes and stories – anything to talk about other than the delay and cause of the delay.

Here are some humorous stories and jokes you can tell to help all relax, and you may want to have a few good stories of your own depending on the people you are playing with and their taste in humor, of course:

Adult Funny Stories and Golf Humor

Here are some humorous adult stories and jokes some of which have been featured in our other books.[32] Share them in your own discretion during any delays on the course, tee backups, and at the Clubhouse bar.

Everyone has their own sense of humor. Some jokes may not be appropriate for some tastes. Some men and women may find these adult jokes offensive. If you do, please skip over them.

Strange Grim Humor. A very avid golfer was playing a private course few golfers ever played and he was elated to play it.

For some unknown reason, he was playing the best golf of his life. He was one under par as he finished the front 9 and was getting ready to tee off on the 10th hole, when his mobile phone began to vibrate.

It was his doctor's office. He'd known the doctor for many years, and the doctor's office was calling him to tell him that his wife had just been in a terrible accident and was in critical condition, and in ICU at the hospital.

The man told the doctor's office to tell the doctor to inform his wife he was at this exclusive golf club, but he'd be there as soon as possible!

As he hung up, he realized he had only 9 holes left, the hospital wasn't that far away, and probably he knew there wasn't much he could do at the hospital anyway. So, he decided to continue to play what was turning out to be the best golf round of his life.

He finished the round with a 79, the lowest score he ever had in his life and was happy he finished.

Then he ran to his car and threw his clubs in the trunk and drove to the hospital still wearing his golf shoes and feeling very guilty.

He parked at the hospital and jogged up to the entrance. As soon as he came through the doors, he saw his doctor standing there. "How is my wife doing?", the golfer asked him.

His doctor, who was a long-time friend of the golfer, glared at him and shouted, "Where were you?! Did you continue to finish your golf round at that fancy golf club?"

The golfer couldn't lie and hung his head nodding that he did continue.

"Well, while you were out enjoying your golf, your wife has been going through a lot in the ICU!"

The doctor continued, "I hope you had a great round because that's the last time you'll be playing golf for a while."

The doctor pointed at the man's golf shoes. "Your wife will require round the clock care from now on, so you won't be doing much else while you'll be caregiving for her."

The golfer was feeling so guilty he broke down sobbing and crying uncontrollably.

The doctor then laughed and said, "I'm just kidding. She's dead. What'd you shoot?"

A golfer was invited to play at his friend's private golf club and during the round he urgently had to urinate.

Realizing he couldn't wait to visit the toilet a few golf holes away, and not wanting to embarrass himself, he noticed a thick stand of trees nearby and ran in and relieved himself behind a tree, thinking no one could see him.

Just at the same time, on an adjacent fairway, three lady members, two brunettes and a blonde were coming down the adjacent fairway, when they observed a penis protruding from around the tree.

"He's not my husband, I'd know if it was him all right," said the first brunette.

"That's disgusting! Look at that! Right on the course. He's not mine either – I'd know his anywhere," said the second brunette.

"Terrible!" Said the blonde. "Why that guy's not even a member here!"

A golfer walks into a barbershop and asks for a shave and a shoeshine.

The barber lathers his face and slowly sharpens his large straight edge on a leather strap, while a beautiful young woman wearing a very low-cut top kneels down in front of him and begins to shine the golfer's shoes.

The golfer's eyes bulge out as he can't help glancing at her large quivering breasts as she brushes his shoes.

The golfer starts to laugh and says to the shoeshine girl, "You and I should get a room."

Completely unfazed, the young beautiful woman says, "My husband wouldn't like that."

The golfer says, "What a waste! Tell your stupid husband you've got to work late, and I'll make it well worth your while."

Unfazed, the beautiful woman continues to brush his shoes, and without looking up says, "You tell him. He's the one shaving you."

That golfer died and was up before God for Judgment. He was met by St. Peter at the Gates of Heaven who greeted him. "Sir, you were a great golfer but before you meet God, I thought I should tell you that other than your great golf career, you really didn't do anything for the common good, or for the bad, so we're not sure what to do with you. We don't have any golf courses in heaven but what particularly did you do on earth that was good?

The golfer pondered for a bit and said, "Once after playing a golf tournament in California, I was driving back to the hotel and there in the parking lot, I saw a young woman being tormented by a group of from a Motorcycle Gang – you know revving their engines, circling her, taunting her with obscenities?"

"Go on," said St. Peter.

"So, I stopped and got out of my car with my 5-iron and went up to the leader – the biggest guy there. He was much bigger than I, very muscular, had tattoos all over, a scar on his face and a ring in his nose. Well, I put my index finger in his nose ring and tore it out of his nose. Then I told him and the rest of them they'd better stop bothering this woman or they all would get more of the same!"

"Wow, that's very impressive sir!" St Peter replied. "When did this happen?"

"About two minutes ago."

Human Nature Humor. PGA Tour Players spend 90% of the year traveling from one tournament to another and spend a lot of time on airplanes.

On an Air India Flight to the US carrying 103 passengers, the crew unfortunately discovered 30 minutes into the flight there were only 40 meals on the plane.

One of the crew assessed the situation advised the passengers, "We apologize to you and we are still trying to figure out how this occurred, but we have about one half of the dinners, eh…, only 40 dinners, and we need to feed the 100 plus passengers on this flight."

After the loud muttering amongst the passengers quieted down, she continued, "Anyone who is kind enough to give up their dinner so someone else could eat, will receive unlimited free alcoholic beverages during the entire duration of the flight."

A second announcement was made an hour and a half later, "If anyone wants to change their mind, we still have 40 dinners available."

After years of traveling on tour, a PGA Tour player finally decided to take a wife and got engaged to a beautiful woman and planned a wedding. They planned to elope to avoid all the wedding publicity.

They were driving to the chapel to get married and they were so excited, the pro golfer drove erratically and crashed his car killing them both. They woke up finding themselves sitting in fluffy white clouds before the gates of Heaven.

They realized they were killed and sat there waiting for St. Peter to open the gates. While waiting, they wondered whether they could get married in heaven by a Catholic priest. St. Peter approached them with his laptop in hand.

"St. Peter," the pro said, "We were wondering if we could get married in heaven?"

St. Peter shook his head, "I don't think we've ever had two people get married in heaven. Wait here, I'll check."

St. Peter went away, and weeks passed. Long lines of people waiting to get into heaven started to form. St Peter was nowhere to be found.

The pro and his fiancé wondered what was going on. They start to have second thoughts about getting married, thinking they might not get along in the eternity ahead, they could have problems with their relationship now that they were going into heaven. They wondered if divorce was allowed in heaven.

Finally, after 10 weeks pass, they see St. Peter walking toward them with his laptop in hand, but he looked very tired and worn out.

"Yep, I'm happy to say, we can arrange for you to get married in Heaven," St. Peter said.

"That's wonderful!" the pro said. "But St. Peter, ah…, while we were waiting, we wondered if our marriage didn't work out, could we get divorced in heaven?"

St Peter looked at the long line of people waiting to get into heaven and started to get angry. He shook his head and walked around in circles a bit, and then said, "Oh Hell! Are you friggin' with me?"

The pro says, "No. Why are you so angry?"

St. Peter opened his laptop and checked on some things. But as he checked he gradually got angrier.

Trying very hard to control his anger, St. Peter kept muttering to himself, "You two are friggin' with me, aren't you?"

"No way," said the pro.

St Peter slammed his laptop down on a cloud and said, "It took me 10 weeks to find a Catholic Priest up here. Do you two have any idea how long it's going to take me to find a lawyer!"

A tough looking woman walked into the golf clubhouse bar and looked around. Filthy, smelly, and wearing ragged clothes, she pounded her fist on the bar, and raised her other arm up in the air exposing a very hairy armpit, and shouted, "Who's going to buy me a stinkin' drink!"

No one in the bar responded. Everyone was trying to ignore her as the club bartender walked over to her to tell her to leave. All at once, old Harry in the back of the bar called out in his old cracking feeble voice, "I'll buy that acrobat a drink."

"Pour me a shot of whisky!" The tough woman said as she pounded her fist on the bar.

The bartender knew old Harry was good for it, so he poured her a shot and she downed it in one gulp. She pounded the shot glass back on the bar and raised her hairy arm pit again and said, "Who's gonna to buy me another friggin' one!"

"I'll buy that acrobat another one," said Harry.

Bartender looked up at Harry and said, "Harry, why the hell do you think this woman's an acrobat?"

"She's got to be an acrobat, since I haven't ever seen a woman raise her leg so high in my life!"

A very elderly Florida grandmother finished shopping and was walking to her car in the parking lot when she noticed 4 young men getting into her car trying to drive it away.

For protection, the elderly lady carried a handgun and when she saw the young men stealing her car, she dropped her bags and pulled out her handgun and started screaming, "Get away from my car! I've got a gun!"

The four young men jumped out of the car and ran like hell.

The incident so shook the elderly woman, she couldn't get her key into the ignition. She kept fumbling and fumbling with her keys and couldn't start the car.

As she started to calm down, she noticed a soccer ball, a baseball cap, and two six packs of beer on the passenger seat next to her.

She got out and realized her car was parked 5 spaces down.

She went to the Police Station anyway and reported the incident to the desk sergeant who couldn't control his laughter.

As the sergeant was trying to catch his breath, he pointed to 4 young men who had just come in to report a carjacking by a crazy old lady, who was waving a huge gun at them. No charges were filed.

An elderly couple were playing a golf course they hadn't played in years. The last time they played this course was at a time when they were in their twenties. There weren't any other golfers playing the course they could see, so they took their time walking the course and reminiscing.

As they played the course, they came across a heavily bushed area where they had sex when they were young, and with devilish smiles they decided to relive it.

The couple went into the bushes and began bonking standing up, then the husband, all at once, started bonking his wife furiously like a rabbit on fire! They were at it over thirty minutes, non-stop!

155

Then they both fell to the ground completely exhausted.

"Holy golf balls!" She said. "You hadn't given it to me like that in 40 years!"

"Forty years ago, that fence wasn't friggin' electric!"

Two very old retired lawyers went golfing and both severely sliced their drives. They were deep in the rough searching for their errant tee shots. Neither of them wanted to lose a new ball so they searched and searched and eventually wandered off the golf course and came upon a pair of tracks.

They stopped and examined the tracks closely. The first old lawyer announced, "My ball hit these tracks and probably rolled down this way somewhere and I'm going to follow these tracks."

The second old lawyer responded, "Our golf balls couldn't possibly go that way down these tracks – at least not very far. I'm not going to waste my time or this golf round searching for your fucking ball in that direction. Besides any idiot could easily see by looking at the level of the land, our balls probably went the opposite way!"

Each old attorney believed himself to have the superior analysis of the situation, and they both bitterly argued on and on. Neither of them would back off from their argument, and they were still arguing heavily when the train hit them.

An old man in an assisted living facility tells the head nurse, "My penis just died."

"Oh, we're so sorry to hear that, Mr. Johnson. May your penis rest in peace."

"Yes, my penis and I had lots of fun together. It was the best club in my golf bag! Haha!"

The next day, Mr. Johnson is walking the halls with his penis hanging out of his pajamas. The nurse scratches her head and approaches him and says, "Mr. Johnson, you told us your penis had died?"

"Yes, rest its soul. Today is the viewing."

A young golfer was hitting balls on a range trying to get the attention of Gary Player who was hitting on the other side of the range. Every time Gary Player would hit a ball the young golfer hit it further then watched Gary to see if he was impressed.

Gary would hit a fade then the young golfer hit a higher and perfect fade even further, and so on. This started to annoy Gary, so he waved the young golfer over to him.

"You hit some impressive shots for a youngster. I was wondering if you've got your tour card yet."

"Well, ah, I could get it any time, I was leading in the last three qualifiers but thought, hey, it's too easy. All that travel? Nope, not for me yet, even though I could qualify any time I choose. I'm going to have fun before I get into that grind."

Player stared at him, and then said, "You know I've designed many golf courses, and I could get you a job at one of the most exclusive courses I've ever designed. They pay around $200k for a new assistant pro. And, the course is owned by a very wealthy old man who is looking for a chauffeur and a bodyguard for his beautiful granddaughter and you'll have to see to all her needs. You're young and very tall and I assume you've got a strong sex drive, because from what I hear, and I don't mean to be awkward but, you're going to need it with this job."

"Yeah, yeah, I got a sex drive!" Said the young golfer, now getting really excited.

"Well you'll have to fly over to South Africa to meet everyone, but the owner will send his jet for you and his granddaughter will come to meet you. She's in her early 20s and she's got one hell of a sex drive. Oh, and you'll have to escort her on all her trips," said Gary.

The young golfer, now wide-eyed, said, "You bullshittin' me?"

Gary replied, "Yeah, well…. You started it."

A New Yorker and a Texan, both high handicappers, were spraying their shots and as a result the Texan had to drive and bounce the golf cart through very rough terrain trying to find their golf balls.

It got so bumpy the New Yorker kept hitting his head on the cart's roof and eventually fell out of the cart.

"Hey, take it easy man. This ain't a rodeo," the New Yorker said as he got up rubbing the top of his head.

"Shit, pardner, you ought to learn bronc riding," said the Texan.

The New Yorker said, "Sounds great but there's no rodeos in the Big Apple."

"You don't need a rodeo. Just get your girlfriend down on her hands and knees, then ride up on her, if you know what I mean. Then reach round and cup both of her breasts and whisper, 'Your sister has bigger ones', then try to hold on for eight seconds!"

A golfer named Frank, passed away and his wishes were to have his ashes scattered in the sea off the coast of California. He loved to drink Scotch, and he directed in his will when his ashes were scattered, every adult in the boat would have a glass of his favorite Scotch, and toast in his honor as his ashes were scattered.

The wind was strong the day his ashes were scattered. One of his friends even became seasick it was so rough.

When it came time to scatter his ashes, the scotch glasses were raised, but instead of the good Reverend scattering his ashes into the sea, the ashes were blown by the strong wind into most of the raised scotch glasses.

The mourners grimaced at ashes floating in their scotch. One of the mourners broke the silence by saying, "Frank's still drinking his favorite scotch!"

A foursome was out playing a golf course with a par three hole which featured a live volcano in the South Pacific.

Only three of them finished the round. The club pro came out and asked where Harry was?

One of them sadly said, "He hit it close to the crater. Suddenly, we heard sounds like heavy seas swishing and crashing against the rocks, then a great rumble, then the ground shook, then we heard a great hissing sound, then a large boulder as big as a pickup truck came flying out of the crater about 100 feet right above Harry."

"Didn't he get out of the way," the club pro asked?

"He looked up at the boulder…his last words were, 'What the f@#k?'… then the boulder came down and squashed him flat as a pancake."

"Shit! I'll get out there right away!"

"Don't bother, we don't need a ruling. The boulder sent his ball flying on the green and into the hole and we already gave him a birdie."

After finishing their round on the Old Course at St. Andrews, 4 golfers went up to the bar on the top floor of a hotel overlooking the course for refreshments.

They sat down at a table and decided to do a 7-whiskey tasting ranging from very smooth scotches (which go down as easy as a glass of water), to smoky, peaty scotches. After tasting 7 whiskeys, they were all well-oiled.

One of the guys got up and walked around to the bar, then noticed a locked cabinet with iron bars and complex combination locks. Surveillance cameras hanging from the ceiling were positioned on it. The guy said, "Bartender, what's in that cabinet?"

"That, my dear sir, is an extremely rare bottle of scotch known as the infamous, "Esmeralda's Islay". It's on loan to us for a few days. There are none better."

"Can I see it?" asked the guy.

The bartender paused, then motioned to a uniformed guard wearing white gloves who opened the cabinet and brought out the beautiful bottle on its elaborate display stand.

The guy bent over to get a closer look at it and let out a fart. The guy nervously glanced around to see if anyone noticed his fart, but the bartender and guard were total professionals and acted like nothing happened.

Embarrassed, the guy moved to another seat pretending to get a better view of the beautiful English Crystal Decanter covered in gold and diamonds. Then says, "How much is it?"

The bartender replied, "My good sir, if you farted just looking at it, you're going to shit yourself when I tell you the price."

John staggered in the door late in the evening after an afternoon round of golf with several beers, then had a big dinner at a Mexican Restaurant, with 7 more beers and 5 Tequilas to wash it all down.

"I'm bushed honey, I'm going to bed early," John said to his wife. He went to sleep but woke up and saw a white-haired man in white flowing robes standing at the end of his bed.

"What the hell? Who are you in my bedroom?" John said.

"This isn't your bedroom, John. Yes, you guessed it, I'm St. Peter and these are at the Pearly Gates."

"What! I can't be dead? Send me back right now!"

"Sorry John, it's not that easy. We don't usually send them back, but I can send you back as a cat or a hen. It's your choice," St. Peter said.

John thought about it. He didn't like cats, and being a hen didn't seem that great either, but it was his only other choice.

"I want to go back as a hen," said John.

Instantly, John is on a farm walking around with other hens on a bright sunny day. He likes the sunshine and nice weather and is enjoying himself.

Another hen walks up to him and says, "You must be the new hen St. Peter told us about. How's it going?"

"Well it's okay, but I feel like my ass is about to explode."

"Oh, that's just the ovulation going on, you've got to lay an egg," says the hen.

"Okay," says John, "How do I lay an egg?"

"Well, when you feel it coming on, let out a cluck and push."

John clucks and pushes. An amazing egg comes out!

"Hey that felt really great," John says to the other hen.

John feels the urge again, pushes, and another egg pops out!

He does it again, and then hears his wife shouting:

"John! Wake up! You're shitting all over the bed!

Joe was a model husband. He worked long hours for a large accounting firm trying to make partner and get as much business and revenue as he could for the firm. Trying to stay fit, Joe religiously went to the gym two nights a week, and he plays golf every Saturday.

His wife of two years was happy he was such a determined man, but she wanted him to relax more. She decided to surprise him and take for his birthday to a local Gentleman's Club one evening. When they drove up, the parking valet at the Club opened the door for Joe's wife. He then went around and took the keys from Joe.

"Nice to see you again, Joe." The parking valet said.

His wife wondered, "Joe, have you been here before?"

"No, haven't ever been here. That guy goes to the same gym I do."

They get a table up front and the waitress brings Joe a bourbon and water. "Here's your usual Joe, what would your guest like to drink?"

Joe's wife orders a wine, then says, "How'd she know you like bourbon and water?"

"She's a bartender at the golf course and knows that's what I drink, sweetheart."

A dancer comes up to their table and rubs her breasts in Joe's face while mussing his hair with both hands and says, "Hi Joey, you want your usual lap dance tonight?"

Joe's wife is fuming and grabs her purse and storms out the door. She waves a taxi down outside. Joe follows her and just gets into the taxi before his wife can slam the door on him. Joe begins pleading with his wife explaining the dancer must have mistaken him for someone else. He begs her to understand. Joe's wife is going bezerk, yelling at him non-stop. She's using every four-letter expletive known to man. Joe continues pleading when the taxi driver turns around and says, "You picked up a real bitch this time, Joe."

After weeks of suspicion, Dorothy, a very jealous wife whose husband always seemed to be playing golf and working late, fired their very attractive maid.

As the beautiful maid was leaving, she said, "Your husband told me that I'm a better golfer than you are."

The jealous wife shrugged her indifference.

"I'm also better in the sack," said the maid.

"My husband told you that?!" Dorothy screamed!

"No, the pool maintenance guy did."

If one of your regular group has bought a brand new super driver and has let everyone on earth know about it (especially if he bought it on sale), there's an old well-known prank that still brings a lot of laughs.

Take an old wooden scratched driver – the most hideous one you come across (perhaps the pro shop might have an old, decrepit driver in the back – one with cobwebs on it in the Lost and Found Bin), and while your friend is distracted, or, in the toilet, etc., take the brand-new head cover off his new driver, and put the new head cover on the decrepit driver and stick it in his bag.

Carefully hide his new driver under another head cover in his own bag or your bag or wherever you can keep it absolutely safe. Have a good laugh when he discovers it.

A golfer's wife says to him, "Sweetheart, I have to confess when I'm having sex with you, I think about other men."

The golfer was reading a book, and without lifting his eyes, said, "Oh, you don't think of me? Well, when I have sex with other women, I'm thinking about you."

The golfer walks very strange now but should be back to his old self once his injuries heal.

Gross Humor. An American golfer and a Costa Rican golfer were playing a golf course in Costa Rica. While putting on the 6th green a group of monkeys gathered on the edge to watch them putt.

Just as the American was about to putt, a bug flew in his ear and he pulled and poked at his ear to get it out.

Suddenly, the group of monkeys went crazy and jumped on the American and beating on him and jumping on him screaming and yelling.

The monkeys ran off and the American stood up in a daze, scratching his head completely puzzled about what just happened.

The Costa Rican golfer explained pulling your ear means, "F#ck You!" in monkey language. The American was angry and vowed revenge.

The next day the American purchased large knives, party hats, party horns, and a large sausage.

He put the sausage in his pants and took it all to the 6th green where the monkeys gathered again to watch him. He tossed several party hats, knives, and party horns to the monkeys, keeping one set for himself.

Knowing that monkeys mimic everything, the American put on a party hat.

The monkeys looked at him, then put on the party hats.

Next, the American picked up his horn and blew on it. The monkeys picked up their horns and did the same.

The American grabbed his knife and the sausage in his pants and sliced it through.

The monkeys looked at the knives, looked at their crotches, looked at the American, and pulled their ears.

A blonde, redhead and a brunette are teeing up on a mountain top tee box when a thunderstorm rolls in. Lightning blasts are all around them. Then a bolt hits all the three of them, and in an instant all three are standing in front of the Gates of Heaven.

St. Peter is standing in front of the gates and says, "If you want to get through these Pearly Gates you have to pass the 100-joke test without laughing."

The redhead hears 37 jokes but can't hold back her laughter anymore, so St. Peter says, "Sorry, you've got to go to hell." And she drops down out of the clouds into a blazing inferno.

The brunette gets all the way up to the 79th joke but likewise busts out laughing and goes to hell.

The blonde listens intently and suddenly as she hears the 99th joke, she busts out laughing and she's laughing so hard she can hardly breathe.

St. Peter stands there scratching his head and says, "The 99th joke is the worst joke of the bunch and you were so close to getting through these Gates, why did you laugh at it?"

Blonde says, "The first joke! I just got it!"

Tiger Woods went into a Spanish bar and sat down next to Sergio Garcia who was chewing gum. Sergio, in between chews, said, "You Americans think you're so great."

"Nope we don't think that," Tiger replied. "I enjoy Spanish food very much, especially paella."

Sergio sneered, "Ha! You Americas are too fat! You eat too much bread."

"Oh yes, we love to eat bread," replied Tiger. "Of course, we eat the inside of the bread and take the outside and recycle it then make cereal with it for Spain."

Sergio, still chomping away on the gum asked, "You Americans eat too many bananas like the monkeys."

Tiger still cool replied, "Well of course we eat bananas and recycle the peels and make smoothies for Spain."

Sergio, still chewing away and clicking the gum, "I hear you are a sexual experto. But Americans do not know how to have good safe sex."

Tiger unfazed, said, "Oh, we use condoms for sex and when we finish with them we recycle them and make gum for Spain."

There are jokes which are so dumb they're funny:

John Daly walks into a bar and gets a beer and notices there's a basket of roasted peanuts in the shell in front of him. John reaches for one, then hears a voice, "You are amazing, John, you hit drives far and you're the man who started the big driving craze, you're good looking too."

John pulls his hand back and takes a sip of beer wondering about what just happened. He tries to get another peanut and hears, "Say you're really looking good, John. You've been working out?"

Then he hears several voices, "That's John Daly! What a guy! He's very smooth! No woman can tame him – he's a big lion! What a catch he is!"

John looks over at the bartender and says, "What the hell? There's voices coming out of the fuc#ing peanut basket?" Bartender says, "Don't worry about it. The peanuts are complimentary."

During the 2008 Economic crisis in the US, two golf course owners were going out of business. One of them asked the other, "Do you pay your employees?"

The other replied, "No, I haven't paid them for months."

"And they still come to work for you?"

"Yes, they come to work."

The other golf course owner said, "My employees come to work too even though I don't pay them either. We should try charging them money for coming to work."

One month later, they meet again. The first golf course owner says, "My employees quit when I started charging them. Did your employees keep working after you charged them?"

"Yes, they keep working but these bastards are trying to save money."

"What do you mean?"

They come to work on Monday and I charge them, but they don't leave until Friday!"

A Bishop, a Minister and a Rabbi went golfing on a very hot and humid day.

It was so hot, they thought they were the only ones on the course. Perspiring profusely, they came up to a clear small river running through the middle of the fairway.

The Bishop said, "I've got to cool off." So, he took his clothes off and jumped into the water. "Ah, that's refreshing!" the Bishop said as he cooled off in the water.

The Minister and the Rabbi likewise took their clothes off and jumped in as well.

They all felt better, but as they were climbing out of the river, a foursome of ladies walked by.

They scrambled for their clothes but were only able to grab their shirts as the ladies passed by. The Bishop and Minister covered their genitals. The Rabbi covered his face instead.

The Bishop and the Minister sheepishly grinned at the ladies as they passed them. The Bishop asked the Rabbi, "Why did you cover your face rather than your genitals?

175

The Rabbi said, "Well, in my Synagogue, they know me by my face, and now I'm not sure about you two."

A Tour pro returned to his Florida home for the Christmas holiday. He'd been away for weeks and after catching up with his family, his 15-year-old son pleaded with him for permission to drive the car.

"I'll make you a deal son, you bring your grades up from a C student to a B student, go to church every Sunday, read the Bible and get a friggin' haircut, and then we'll talk about driving.

When the touring pro came back home two months later, his son's grades were at an A-minus average, and he'd studied the Bible every day. The pro, however, said, "I'm disappointed you didn't get your hair cut?"

"Hey! I went to church every Sunday, read the Bible, and most of the people in the Bible had longer hair – a lot longer than mine! Samson had very long hair, Moses too. All the Apostles had long hair, hell everyone had long hair, the son replied.

"Yeah, but did you notice they walked everywhere they went?"

That's a bad joke, Dad.

The same Tour pro came home a few months later and had just come in from a long late flight. He crept softly into the house. He didn't want to wake anyone. He quietly went to check on his son but was shocked when he saw his son's bed was still made and his son was gone!

There was an ominous envelope propped up on the pillow which was addressed to "Dad."

Thinking the worst, he tore open the letter and read it with shaking hands.

"Dear Dad,

I'm sorry to write this letter and the worries it brings but I've gone off to marry my new girlfriend, Bubbles. I know you and Mom wouldn't approve of her.

I'm in love with Bubbles very much. She's a lot older than me but she loves me a lot and I love her very much too. She's a dancer at the gentleman's club and knows how to please a man.

But it's not only the sex and all the alcohol we drink, Dad. She's pregnant. I'm not sure if I'm the father, but Bubbles says I am and we will be very happy.

She and I are off to live in a commune in Zimbabwe and that's where we are off to and we are going to have many more children. She's got two other kids already.

Bubbles tells me marijuana and the other drugs really don't hurt you. We smoke it a lot, and the methamphetamines she gives me give me a lot of energy. I'm going to learn how to make it too!

Don't worry Dad, I know I'm only 15, but I can take care of myself and her and your future grandchild. When I get back, we'll probably have lots of grandchildren for you and Mom to enjoy.

Love,

Joey

P.S. Dad, this isn't true. I'm over at Ted's house tonight. There are worse things in life than not getting a haircut. I'm going to learn to drive eventually? Hope you didn't become very angry reading this?

Joe was having a terrible day on the course. He was playing foursomes in teams of two and caused a loss on almost every hole. After he missed a one-foot putt to lose another hole, his partner asked him,

"This isn't like you, Joe. You make those one-footers in your sleep. What's going on with you?"

"Shit! It's the wife" said Joe. "As you know, she's taken up golf, and says she loves the game – she's always gone. And, ever since she's been playing, she's cut my sex down to once a week."

A guy on the other team overheard and said, "You should consider yourself really lucky, Joe,"

"What do you mean?" Joe asked.

"Hell, she's cut some of us out altogether!"

A series of lessons is the best way to learn golf. But, very few can learn golf in one lesson.

Have you heard the story about a pro shop sign that read?

"One Golf Lesson $10,000

Five Golf Lessons $200

If you want a miracle, you have to pay for it."

A man was rushed into the emergency room needing surgery on his penis.

The ER physician examined him and asked, "What the hell happened?"

"Well, doc, I've been a member of the Fireside Golf Club for several years and there's this beautiful blond waitress in the clubhouse. She's blonde and built, a beautiful and curvaceous woman. She's got a problem since she's so horny that every time she goes back in the kitchen, she masturbates with a sausage. She sticks it in a hole on a bench, then she goes up and down and masturbates herself on it."

"And?" asked the doctor.

"Well, I felt this was a waste, so I got under the bench and when she put the sausage in the hole, I removed it and substituted my penis."

"It was a great idea, and everything was going well. Then someone came in the kitchen and she tried to hide by taking a hammer pretending she was tenderizing it for the skillet."

Seven Special Golf Tips:

1. Don't have any more than 37 golf tips in your conscious thoughts as you start your downswing at the ball.

2. Unless you are brain dead or a stoic sociopath, remember the shit wagon follows the mayor's parade. After you make a birdie, expect a triple bogey or worse on the next hole. To keep the shit wagon from following you, keep saying to yourself, "I am not good or bad. I am not good or bad. I am not good or bad...."

3. Putts that are six inches short rarely go into the hole. If you should see one go in, jump out of bed. Your alarm didn't go off, and you're late for your tee time.

4. Know you can easily hit a fairway a mile wide one out of ten times. Know you can hit any leaf on a tree branch nine out of ten times.

5. Know any golf lesson temporarily corrects errors you will regain after three rounds of golf. Only then can you return to your trusted and reliable ways.

6. Any player who searches for his own ball and waives off any assistance, will find his ball.

7. Once you shake hands on the 10th green after losing in match play, you will win every single one of the rest of the eight holes.

A large bus hit an engineer and the next thing he knew he was standing before St. Peter in front of the pearly gates.

St. Peter was sitting at a desk going over things on his laptop. The engineer cleared his throat to get his attention. St. Peter looked up.

"Ah, you're the engineer — I see here you've been assigned to hell."

In an instant, the engineer is standing before a fiery cave and greeted by Satan himself.

Satan is holding a pitch for with one hand and points the engineer with his other hand to a large cave with flames shooting out of it. The engineer walked into the cave.

After a while, the engineer gets bored with the place, so he designs and implements building improvements.

The engineer designs new land use designs to construct large developments. He puts in air conditioning in all structures, etc. Eventually, everyone in hell has a massive home with refrigerators, large swimming pools and waterfalls. The engineer becomes very popular.

One day, God calls up Satan and asks, "How's it all burning down there in hell?"

"Hey, things are fantastic!" Satan says, "We've got brand new residences with full air conditioning, swimming pools, hey, the engineer is great!"

"What the hell? An engineer? There in hell? St. Peter must have screwed up again! Send that engineer back to heaven immediately." God said.

"No way! Everybody likes this guy, and I like this guy! And, I'm not letting him out of here." Satan said.

"Oh, yeah? How'd you like a thunderbolt up your arse!"

"I'd just jump in my pool, Haha!" Satan laughed.

"Listen you demon, you send him back up here or I'll sue you!" God said.

"Haha! Yeah right. You got lawyers up there… Haha…."

A Fictitious Joke: Tiger Woods decided to get married to a wonderful woman and they were deeply in love. He proposed, and she accepted, and they planned a large beautiful wedding.

At an extravagant wedding ceremony in a huge Church, the soft-spoken minister began the marriage ceremony. The Church became silent. The minister routinely asked if anyone in the temple had anything to say or a reason the two should not get married, "Speak now, or forever hold your peace," the minister said.

There was a quick moment of utter silence which was broken like the blade of a pitching wedge striking a rock, when a beautiful young woman carrying a newborn baby stood up in the last pew and started walking toward the minister slowly.

The newborn's cries and whimpers echoed as the young girl continued to approach the front of the church.

Chaos ensued quickly. The bride threw her flowers in Tiger's face. The groomsmen winked at each other, and the wide-eyed bridesmaids couldn't believe what they were witnessing.

The bride's father got up and took a wild swing at Tiger, then put his arm around his daughter, and took her out of the church.

Tiger couldn't believe what was happening but stood his ground as the young woman and newborn approached him and the minister.

Most of the wedding guests got up and began to head for the exits.

The minister asked the woman, "My dear woman, why on earth did you come up here? What is your reason?"

The young woman replied, "We can't hear anything way in the back of the church."

A young golf pro returned from his honeymoon with his new bride, but they weren't talking to each other. Not one bit.

The pro went to work the next day and his boss asked him, "How the honeymoon go?"

"Okay at first, but I was single for a long time and wasn't getting used to it yet."

"What do you mean 'Not used to it'?" Said his boss.

"After we finished having sex, I put a $100 bill on the pillow – it was just habit and I didn't think twice about it."

"Wow, you are definitely in trouble. Maybe your wife will feel better with time?"

"Hell, I'm not concerned about her. The problem I have is she left $90 change!"

Finally, if someone's been on your case, or unnecessarily annoying you, you can play this joke on him during drinks after a round of golf.

Tell the others in your group beforehand about the prank, and the more he's been annoying you, the funnier the prank will be.

Present him with a challenge that he can't balance two mugs of beer on the back of both of his hands at the same time for 10 minutes. If he takes you up on it, you are in for a lot of laughs.

If he accepts the challenge, order two mugs of beer and tell him to put both of his palms face down on the table. Carefully place two mugs of beer on the back of his hands. Bet him free beers, 10 dollars, or whatever you like, he can't balance the two mugs of beer for more than 10 minutes on the back of his hands without spilling a drop.

Once the mugs are balanced on the back of his hands, you and the others in your group should randomly leave the table and move to another table.

If you do this prank near the end of drinks, you and the others could even walk out the door (making excuses you're going to the toilet, check something out, etc.), and leave him there having to pay the bar tab as well.

You might be able to better persuade him to take the bet after he's had a few when it's nearing the end of the drinks.

This is also an excellent prank to play on someone who habitually mooches, e.g., avoids paying for drinks (even though he can well afford to buy drinks for others) and relies on others to pay for the drinks.

Once you tell a joke or two, the others in the group will begin telling their jokes, and next thing you know, you'll be teeing up to play again.

What To Do When Playing Behind a Slow Group That Won't Let You Play Through

Again, it's most important to relax and not tense up. You can, of course, ask the slow group politely to play through, or call the pro shop and tell them to send the ranger out to tell them they must let your group through. If there is an empty hole ahead of the slow group, golf etiquette requires them to allow your group to play through.

So, instead:

1. Think of something pleasant like a fun evening you may have planned, or a nice event you're looking forward to in the future – anything but golf and give your mind a rest.

2. Do slow relaxed practice swings keeping an even tempo and your muscles relaxed.

3. Talk about anything else with the other players in your group. If another player in your group is agitated, leave him alone – he doesn't need any more thoughts to crowd his agitated brain.

4. Have a drink out of your cart cooler. Or, wave down the drink cart girl, and strike up a conversation.

Things To Do When Playing With An Annoying Player.

Say, one of your group is unusually slow, having a bad day, starts to complain about everything, or for whatever reason, is causing you or others to lose the tempo of play. It might be he's got something else bothering him, and if he shares it with you, that will help him get back on track.

Don't tell him he should speed up his play. That will complicate things more for him. His brain is probably going 60mph anyway, and he doesn't need more to think about.

If he asks you for help, offer encouraging advice and tell him what you think might make him play better and faster in a tactful way. Or, if you do see something that would be helpful, volunteer it to him in a friendly, sincere, and encouraging way.

Quick Tips When You Think Your Golf Can't Get Any Worse

Have you ever been in a round when for reasons unknown, you start shanking and mishitting the ball and have no idea what's causing the bad play?

Most of the time, it's due to the fact you are a casual golfer who doesn't practice the game every day.

Or, during your round, perhaps something upset you causing you stress which makes a smooth coordinated golf swing very difficult to execute.

How To Play Better and Have More Fun

1. Check your grip. Hold your club in your left hand by your side and rest the club head on the ground. Grasp the club using only the two middle fingers of your left hand. Let your index finger and little finger

just rest on the grip. Then raise the clubhead up parallel to the ground using only your middle two fingers.

When the club is parallel to the ground, softly place your right hand on the grip using an interlocking grip or a Vardon grip.

Or do your usual pre-shot routine paying more attention when you form your grip on the club.

Swing using only 80% power. Your shots should go straighter.

2. Keep your head down when you strike the ball. Outside pressures come and go during a round. Being under any kind of pressure – whether it's desperately trying to win a hole, or whatever, all tend to make you seek relief from the pressure to win by raising your head too quickly looking for a great shot – which isn't going to be there.

Additional pressure develops from playing badly and good shots generally won't happen until you calm yourself down. Remember to do your pre-shot routine before you take your stance.

3. Don't bet if you can't afford it. Losing bets in a golf round isn't fun. There's no shame in announcing you only want to bet up to a certain

amount. If you bet too much, that's a great way to lose friends.

4. Don't keep score. Not keeping score releases all mental pressure to score well. It's a good change of pace to see yourself make quality shots when it doesn't matter if you score well or not.

5. Concede any putt that's within the length of the flagstick (USGA recommends flagsticks to be at least 7 feet). Missing a 5-footer or less can be extremely aggravating, like the old joke:

"A masochist and a sadist teamed up for a Two-Man Better Ball tournament, and they almost won the whole tournament! But, the masochist missed a very easy and simple one-foot putt they needed on the 18th green, and lost it all for the twosome.

The masochist pleaded and pleaded with his sadist partner, 'Please hurt me... hurt me for missing that short putt!'

"No," replied the sadist."

There are many who say you need to hole out every putt to stay sharp and practice your ability to make short putts. But, just for once, play a round where you concede any putt less than the length of the flagstick – i.e., 7 feet or less. Of course, you can't record the score, but it makes the round a lot more enjoyable and less aggravating.

Another spinoff of conceding putts within flagstick length, is to agree before you start your social round of golf, that no one is allowed more than three putts. In other words, if any player misses his second putt, he can pick up since the third putt is conceded no matter how long it is. This will also speed up your group's play.

6. Bring a speaker and play your music. You can use headphones or put a small speaker in your golf cart to listen to your music during a round so long as it doesn't distract anyone. Music is a great way to relax as well as keep your good energy flowing. Your music should help you to maintain a fluid golf swing too.

7. Play a 9 hole or 18-hole golf round by yourself. A solo walk on an uncrowded course during summer early evening is a relaxing and enjoyable experience.

8. Use two balls when you play alone. You can play a solo Ambrose (hit two balls and chose the best one, then hit two balls from there, and so on until

you hole out). You play the better of the two shots and see what you score – kind of like giving yourself a mulligan every shot.

Or, you can play two balls and see if you score better on your first ball vs. the second ball.

9. If you play in a regular foursome in a private club every week, play a different course for a change of pace. If your club has reciprocal rights to play on another course, plan a road trip, and stop for a nice breakfast along the way, for a change of pace.

10. Get better at your short game. If you are a high handicap golfer over 50, the best way to improve scoring is to improve your short game.

As in the adage, "You only get out what you put into it," take a lesson(s) from a golf professional just on the short game. Practice as much as you can on a regular basis and see if your scoring dramatically improves.

Ray Floyd grew up on a golf course his father owned, and Ray spent a lot of time practicing his short game around the green.

We contacted Ray and asked him what his advice would be to score better. He emailed us, "My advice to any golfer who wants to excel at the sport is to dedicate yourself to being good in all aspects of the game."

Ray wrote, "Everyone, likes to hit the ball hard and long. But that goes away as you live longer."

"The real scoring part takes place from 60 yards in, so I encourage spending as much time learning how to chip and putt."

"The finesse shots around the green and short approaches were one of the real strengths of my game, and in my prime, I felt I could outplay anyone in the game around the green."

Ask your pro to teach you about sand shots, flop shots, chips, bump and runs, the one hop and stop, putting techniques, etc.

If you don't want to spend the money for a golf lesson, there are many videos on the web relating to the short game only. Take one video at a time and practice it until you've mastered it, then go on to the next video.

Our favorite YouTube Video is Phil Mickelson's "Secrets of the Short Game – Part I" which is over an hour in length and had over 1 million views in a little over a year.[33]

11. Play the course in reverse, or in a Cross-country manner. For example, at St. Andrews in Scotland, you can play from the first tee to the 17th green, then play from the 18th tee to the second green, etc. The unusual aspect of playing in reverse is the bunkers and other hazards are facing the opposite way when you play a hole in reverse.

In Cross-country golf, you play from tee boxes to different greens. This results in your having to play precise shots (e.g. hitting through a gap in the tree line) on a course you're familiar with, and wind up approaching the green from a different angle.

Generally, the golf course must arrange and organize a Cross-country or a Reverse Play tournament and should map out the route of play.

It's a fun experience and gives everyone a change of pace, and the golf course gets a lot of word of mouth advertising.

12. If you are playing badly, forget about your total score and concentrate on making the best score you can on each of the remaining holes. For example, say you scored a 9 on the last hole, and the score for your total round is totally shot. As you come up to the next tee box, think back to the best score you've ever made on this next hole. Then

block everything else out of your mind and try to better that score, and so on, until you finish on the 18th hole.

If you better your best score on any of the remaining holes, you should feel good even though you shot a very bad total score for the entire round.

13. If you are just playing bad golf, depart from your normal play and choke down on the grip two to three inches when you use the club. Do that with every club you use from your driver to your putter. A club with a shorter shaft is normally easier to hit than a club with a longer shaft. You may not hit it as far, but you will strike the ball better and produce more accurate online shots to the green.

14. If you are simply playing badly and not having any fun, try to shorten your backswing. Shortening your backswing makes it easier to hit a ball since it forces you to concentrate on your timing and coordination. Your brain will adjust to the shorter backswing, and you'll be having a good time making good contact again.

As a bonus, once you've adjusted to a shorter backswing, you'll probably find you are hitting it farther since your timing will improve, and your total body coordination in striking the ball will result in more distance.

9. GOLF EXERCISE PROGRAMS

There are six basic golf exercise programs that are necessary for golf fitness:

1. Leg Exercises. Strong leg muscles help you do a coordinated golf swing. Besides toning your leg muscles, doing squats with weights will exercise most every muscle in your body.

2. Chest Exercises. Well-toned pectoral muscles are useful as you bring the golf club downward from the top of your golf swing, as well as many other benefits.

3. Back Exercises. Strong back muscles will help protect your spine from injury, especially the lower lumbar region.

4. Core Exercises. A strong core (the muscles around the center of your body), also protect your spine from injury, and helps all aspects of your golf swing.

5. Stretching and Balancing Exercises. Stretching promotes the flexibility needed for a smooth and

fluid golf swing. Balancing exercises are also important as we age, and balancing exercise programs are included to help maintain your vestibular system.

6. Cardio Programs. Helps increase and maintain your stamina to play golf over a 4-5-hour period on the course.

All exercise programs need to be done on a regular basis to be effective, produce results, and protect you against injury.

Greg Norman has a very busy schedule with business commitments. However, his commitment to maintaining his physique is crucial to his business performance, so he regularly sets aside one to two hours a day, five days a week for exercise.

Select two exercises from the first four weight exercise programs (i.e., choose two exercises from the Legs, Chest, Back, and Core Programs) and do these 8 exercises (4 x 2 = 8) at least two days a week.

There are 10 different weight exercises in each of the first four weight exercise programs but select only two of them from each program for the first six weeks. Do at least two gym sessions a week for the first six weeks. Do two sets of 10 reps of each exercise using moderate weights. Limiting each exercise to two sets of 10 reps each will give good muscle tone and avoid overworking your muscles and possible injury from overworking muscles.

Then, every 6 weeks, choose two different exercises from these four weight exercise programs to establish a new 6-week weight routine for a more well-rounded, and more interesting weight exercise program.

Do the Stretching Program for 5-10 minutes at the end of each weight exercise session. You can also add balance training exercises which are also included in this book. Stretching and Balance Training Programs don't take a lot of time to do.

On the other three days when you are not doing weight training exercises, select cardio exercises in the Cardio Program for at least one hour on the other three days.

You can do a third day of weight exercises in each week, but that's optional and up to you. You would then be exercising 6 days a week, if you can schedule it in your weekly schedule.

In any exercise program, you need to keep it interesting to keep yourself motivated to get results. A University of Florida study found if you keep repeating the same routine, your chances of discontinuing your exercise programs increase. Variety is important in an exercise program.[34]

One way to fight boredom is to vary your gym routine every four weeks to six weeks.

If counting reps while your workout gets tiring, try counting reps backward. Or, if you're doing a set of say 10 reps, count in 2 groups of 5-counts to total 10 repetitions, or count backward.

Do supersets, which means after you do one set of an exercise, go right into an opposite exercise without pausing. For example, after doing one set of dumbbell flys for your chest, walk over to the cable machine and without resting, do a set of 10 seated cable rows. Then rest a minute and go back and do another set of dumbbells flys, then an immediate set of cable rows, and so on completing 2 sets of two exercises.

Supersets will keep your heart rate up as well.

Listen to different music in your headphones. That is, keep changing your playlist and add new playlists.

Having a gym workout partner will help to keep things interesting as well. Your partner may be using lighter or heavier weights, but you can motivate each other and have contests between yourselves. For example, see who can hold a plank, or a side plank the longest.

If you and your gym partner are aiming to lose weight, have friendly wagering over who can lose the most weight each week on a percentage basis, i.e., your very own "Biggest Loser" Contest.

Another way to keep things interesting is to set small individual goals for yourself. Seeing your own progress will keep you motivated. Your weight may stay the same but take photos of yourself every three weeks to see your body shape changing. There's a journal in the Appendix of this book for you to keep track of your workouts, weights, etc.

Women, it's up to you on how much weight you want to use but use only very light weights or no weights on a barbell or dumbbell when starting an exercise program for the first time.

Leg Exercises

Squats

Hold two dumbbells of moderate weight in each hand and stand with your feet shoulder width apart with your toes slightly pointed out.

Slowly squat by lowering yourself keeping your back straight as you descend to "sit down".

Squat only as far as you can comfortably. Then in a smooth continuous motion, use your quadriceps to raise yourself back up to the starting position.

Do two sets of 10 reps each. Again, you can do more sets or reps if you like, but keeping the weight moderate and limiting each exercise to two sets of 10 reps each, will give good muscle tone and avoid overworking your muscles, and possible injury.

Smith Machine Squats

Ask for instructions if you are unfamiliar with the Smith Machine.

Begin warming up the leg muscles with a squatting motion with no weights on the bar (use a pad on the bar as well).

Lower yourself by bending at the knees, keeping your back straight.

Descend slowly bending at the knees as if you are sitting down and keep looking forward.

Lower yourself down as far as you comfortably can, then slowly return to the starting position.

Do two sets of 10 reps each.

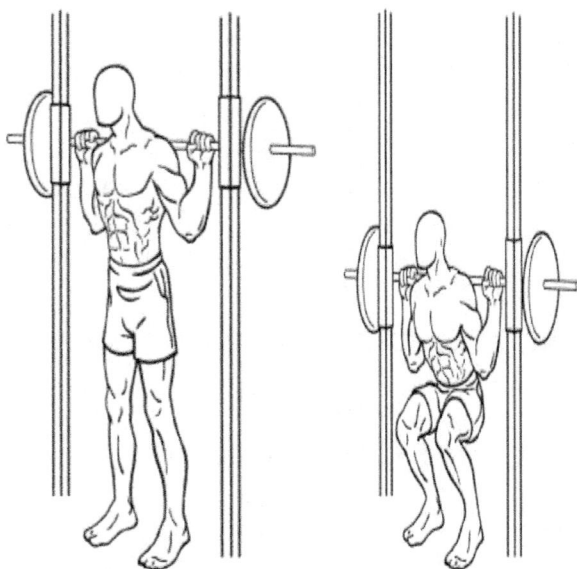

Squats with an Empty Barbell.

Lower yourself by bending at the knees, keeping your back straight, and holding a padded empty barbell on your back shoulders.

Descend slowly bending at the knees as if you are sitting down and keep looking forward.

Lower yourself down as far as you comfortably can, then slowly return to the starting position.

Do two sets of 10 reps each.

Leg Press

Use a leg press machine and ask for instructions if you are unfamiliar with the machine. Adjust the machine to fit your physique. Your feet should reach the foot crosspiece with a slight bend in your knees. Your feet should have a space between them of about a shoulder width apart.

Press your feet forward as there usually are safety locks to release. Release the locks and slowly lower the weight towards your body with your thighs and calves making a 90-degree (or less) angle but only as far as it feels comfortable, then return to the starting position. Don't lock your knees at the top or bounce the platform.

Do two sets of 10 reps each.

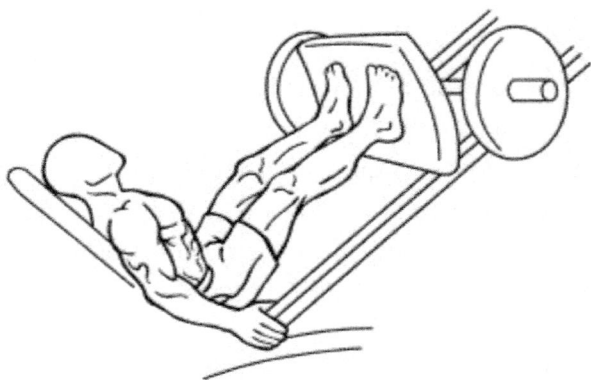

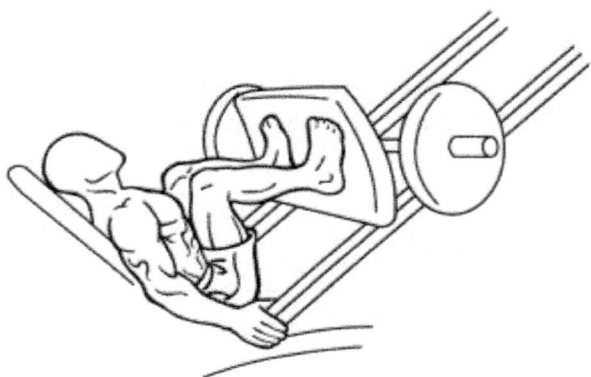

Toe Circles for Calves

Stand on one foot and hold on to a chair or a wall to support yourself.

Lift one of your feet up and make circles with your toes in the air ten times.

Then reverse the direction and draw circles in the other direction 10 times.

Switch feet and do 10 circles with the other foot in each direction. This will stretch and tone your calf muscles and ankles.

Do two sets of 10 reps with each foot.

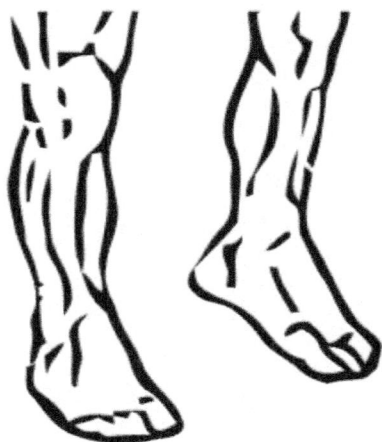

Seated Calf Raises

Using a calf raise machine (get instruction on the machine if you need to) adjust the seat and bar to fit your physique. Raise and lower exercising your calves.

Do two sets of 10 reps each.

Calf Raises Using a Barbell

Many gyms have smaller barbells you can take off the rack with preset weights. Use these preset weight smaller barbells if they feel comfortable, and as always, select a moderate weight.

Place a square block two inches thick or more and sit on a bench holding a barbell on your lower thighs above your knees with the balls of your feet on the block.

Raise and lower the barbell pressing with your toes on the block without lifting your feet off the block.

Do two sets of 10 reps each.

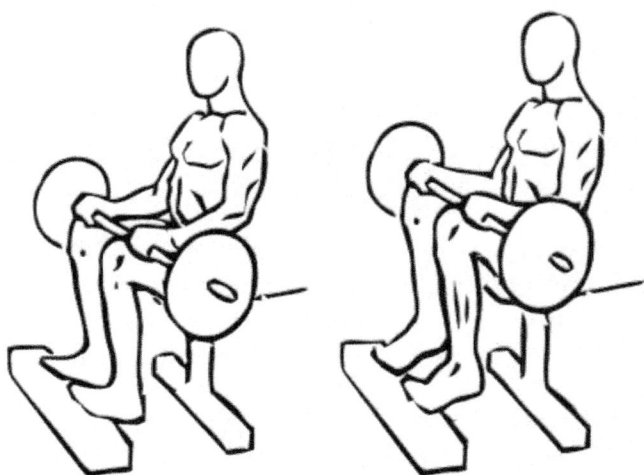

Leg Extensions

Get instruction for the leg extension machine if you are unfamiliar with it and adjust the machine to fit your physique.

Keeping your back flat against the seat, slowly raise up and extend your legs until straight.

Do a slight pause at the top, then slowly lower to the starting position.

Do two sets of 10 reps each.

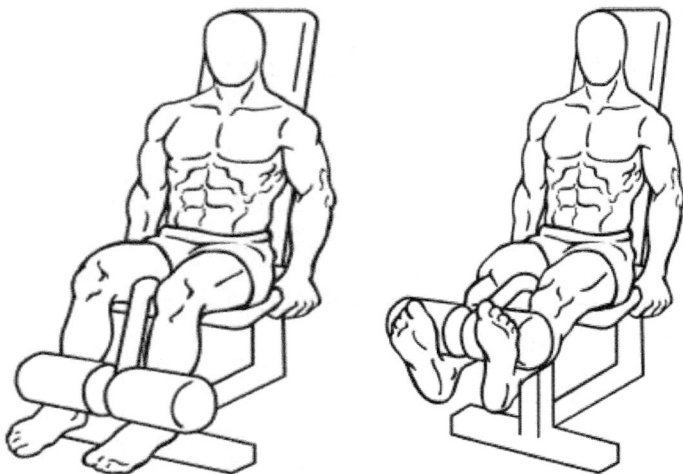

Leg Curls

Get instructions for the machine if you are unfamiliar with it and adjust the machine to fit your physique.

Keep your back straight as you curl your legs back toward yourself and pause for a second, then return to the starting position.

Do two sets of 10 reps each.

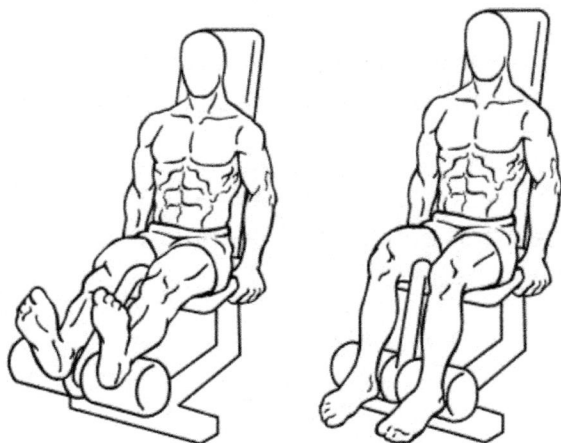

Lunges with Dumbbells

Hold one dumbbell of moderate to light weight in each hand.

Step out in front of yourself with your right leg. The more you step forward, the more difficult the exercise becomes.

As you step forward, lower your left knee down as if genuflecting while lowering your right knee to about a 90-degree angle. Keep your back straight and pause before your knee touches the ground.

Then repeat the lunge stepping out with your left leg and genuflect with your right knee touching the ground.

Alternate the lunges for a total of 5 lunges with each leg.

Do two sets of 5 lunges with each leg or a total of 10 lunges per set.

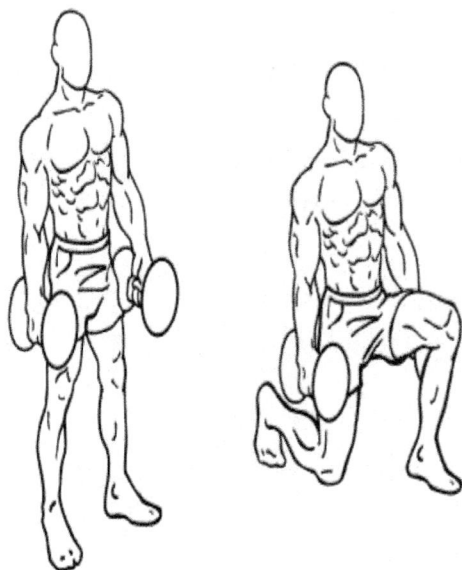

Chest Exercises

Dumbbell Chest Press

Hold a dumbbell of moderate weight in each hand and sit on the bench resting the dumbbells on your thighs. Carefully roll back with the dumbbells and lie on a flat bench with your feet on the ground.

Extend your arms up over your chest keeping your palms facing forwards.

Press the dumbbells up over your chest.

Lower both dumbbells, bending your elbows to a 90-degree angle to a point where your upper arms are parallel with the floor, or as close thereto as you comfortably are able.

Then smoothly raise the dumbbells above your chest.

Keep an even tempo when you raise and lower the dumbbells.

Do 2 sets of 10 reps.

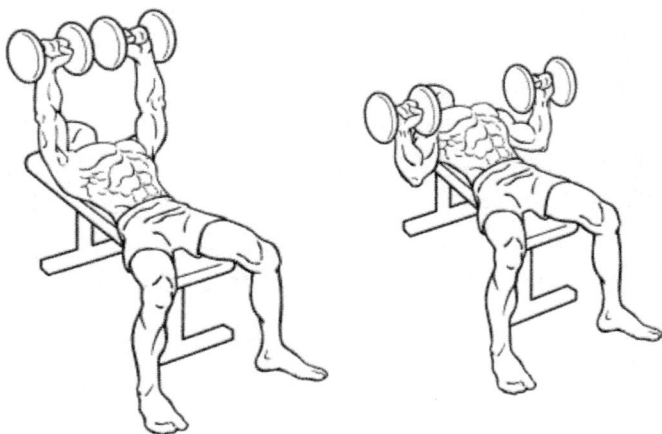

Close Grip Barbell Press – use a spotter

On a flat bench, grasp the barbell with or without weights (use moderate weights you are comfortable with) using a close grip with both hands about 12 to 14 inches apart. Make sure the weights are secure on the bar. Be careful to keep the barbell balanced as you do this exercise and use a spotter.

Raise the barbell off the rest and raise the bar above your chest.

Lower the bar slightly above your chest as far as you comfortably can.

Then return the barbell up above your chest. Keep an even tempo when you raise and lower the bar.

Do two sets of 10 reps.

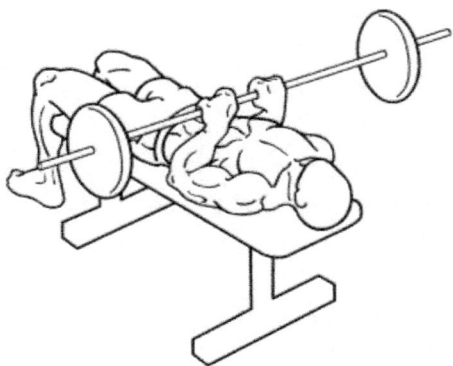

Wide Grip Decline Bench Press

Lie down on a declining bench and have a spotter hand you a light barbell.

Take a wide grip and hold the bar over your chest, then lower it to your chest.

In a continuous motion, raise the bar back up over your chest. Keep an even tempo raising and lowering the barbell.

Do two sets of 10 reps each.

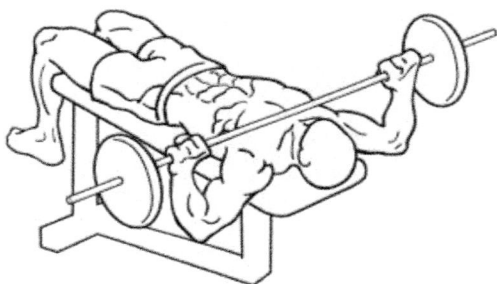

Cable Chest Pull Downs

Adjust the height of two cable pulleys to shoulder height.

Grab the handles – one in each hand and take a step forward. You can place one of your feet slightly in front of the other if it helps you balance better.

Bring your hands together in front of you pulling at a downward angle and pause for a second when your hands meet.

Then in the same tempo you pulled the handles, allow the handles to raise up to where you began the exercise. Repeat.

Do two sets of 10 reps.

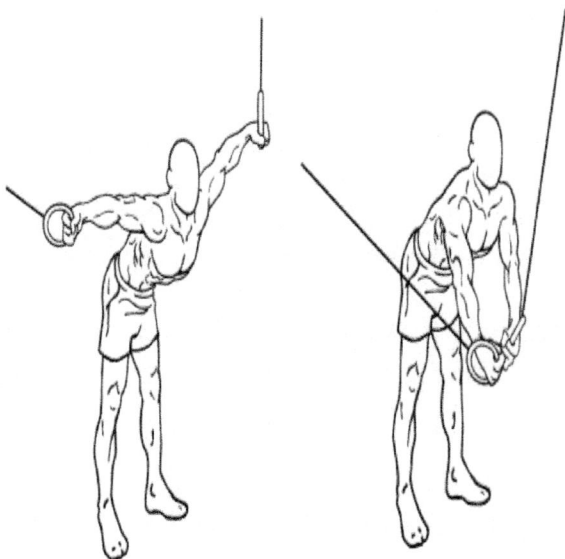

Neutral Grip Incline Dumbbell Press

Lie on an incline bench and adjust it to an incline of about 45 degrees.

Hold both dumbbells with your palms facing each other. Slowly raise your arms up over your chest and in an even tempo, lower the dumbbells to where you began the exercise. Repeat.

Use moderate weights, as always, and do two sets of 10 reps.

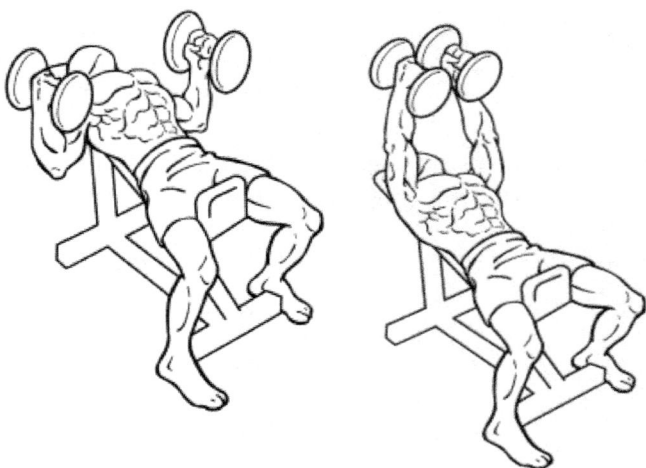

Push Ups

Begin in a raised push up position with your back straight, arms extended, and toes on the floor. Your hands should be outside your shoulders and even with your shoulders.

Using a slow controlled motion, allow yourself to lower to the floor, keeping your back straight, then slowly raise back up.

Do two sets of 10 reps.

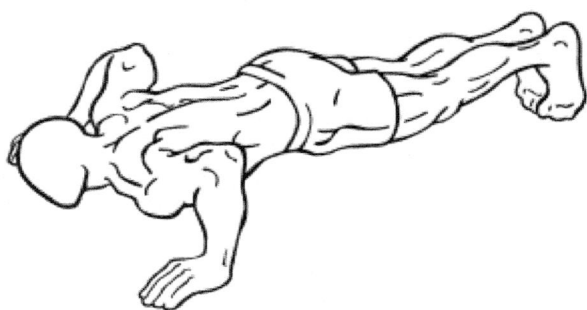

Decline Dumbbell Flys

On a decline bench with your head lower than your body, ask someone to hand you moderate weight dumbbells.

Hold the dumbbells above your shoulders and keeping a slight bend in your elbows, lower the dumbbells down laterally. Don't lower the dumbbells any further if it starts to feel uncomfortable.

Then return to the starting position keeping a slight bend of your elbows at the top.

Do two sets of 10 reps.

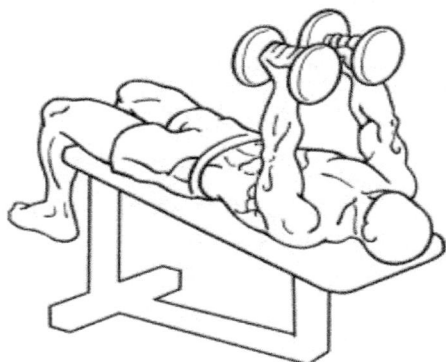

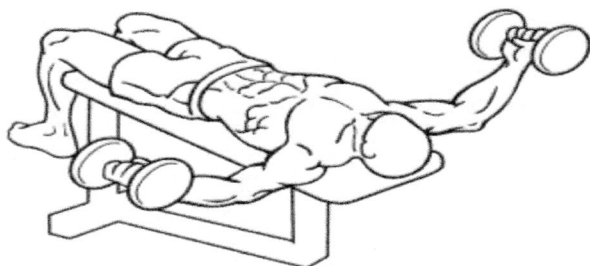

Incline Bench Press

Lie on an incline bench set at about a 45-degree angle and keep your feet shoulder width apart.

Raise the barbell off the rests and hold it over your chest.

Lower the bar down to your chest but don't let it touch your chest.

In one continuous motion raise the bar straight up to where you began the exercise. Repeat.

Do two sets of 10 reps.

You can also do these using a Smith Machine.

Dumbbell Bent Arm Pullover

Pick up a moderate weight dumbbell off the floor and sit on a flat bench. Grasp the dumbbell by the inside plate (making sure the plate(s) is not loose as it could fall on you).

Roll back on a flat bench holding the dumbbell above you over your chest.

Anchor your feet. Lower the dumbbell keeping your arms straight with your elbows slightly bent in an arc over your head and towards the floor.

Then pull the dumbbell back on the same arc above your chest in a slow and controlled manner.

Do two sets of 10 reps.

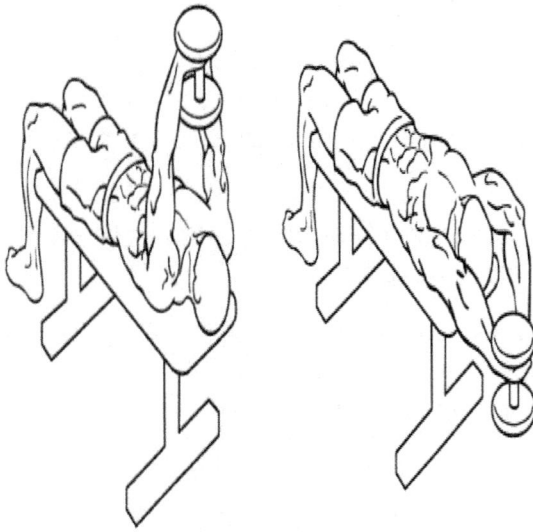

Wide Grip Bench Press

Use a spotter if one is available.

Take a wide grip and lift the bar off the rack as you lay on a flat bench.

Lower the bar, then in one continuous motion, raise the bar back up to where you began the exercise.

Repeat.

Do two sets of 10 reps.

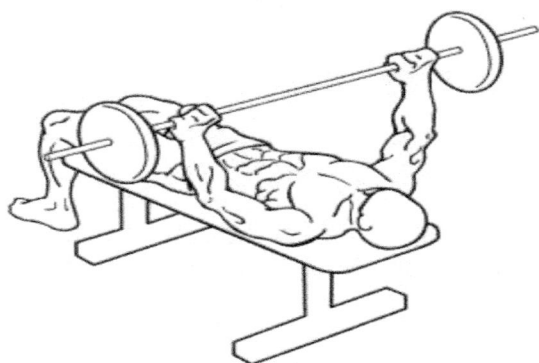

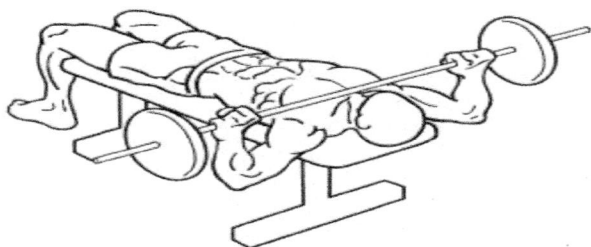

Back Exercises

Back Extensions Using a Swiss Ball

Lie on a Swiss Ball with your toes at least shoulder width apart on the floor for balance.

With your arms on the ball for stability, raise your chest off the ball so you are flexing your back muscles and hold for two seconds.

Lower and repeat.

Do two sets of 10 reps.

Dumbbell Row

Leave a dumbbell on the floor next to a bench and take the position shown in the diagram.

Pick up the dumbbell off the floor using one of your hands.

Raise the dumbbell to chest height, then lower in a smooth continuous motion.

Do one set of 10 reps, then switch arms and do one set of 10 reps with your left arm. Use moderate weight.

Switch back to using your right arm and do one set of 10 reps, then switch arms and do another set of 10 reps with your left arm.

Shoulder Shrugs

Standing with your feet shoulder width apart and a slight bend in your knees, hold a dumbbell of moderate weight in each hand at your sides.

Raise both shoulders up.   Hold for one second, then lower in a smooth and controlled motion.

Do two sets of 10 reps each.

Lat Pull Down

In a sitting position on a lat pull down machine, reach up for the bar using a wide grip with your palms facing forward.

With your back straight, pull the bar down to your upper chest.

Then return the bar smoothly to the top. Repeat.

Do two sets of 10 reps each.

Pull Ups

Pull ups may be difficult but it's great for the back muscles and your abdominals. There may be a pull up machine in the gym which you can adjust to assist you in doing pull ups. Ask for instruction on the pull up machine before you attempt it.

This is a great exercise for your lats, entire middle back and biceps.

Pull yourself up and raise up as high as you comfortably can.

Then lower yourself down to where you began the exercise.

Do as many of these as you can. Don't hold your breath and keep breathing through the exercise. Exhale as you pull yourself up and inhale as you lower yourself.

Body and Back Row

Lie down on the floor below the bar.

Keeping your back flat and using your arms, lift and row your body off the floor towards the bar.

Then lower yourself to the floor.

Repeat.

Start with two sets of 5 reps and work up to 10 reps.

Cable Row

Take a sitting up position on a low cable pulley machine. Place your feet on the footrests with your knees slightly bent.

Lean slightly forward and grab the pulleys with your palms facing each other. Pull the handles back and pause slightly when you bring the handles to your chest, then return to where you began the exercise keeping an even tempo.

Repeat.

Do two sets of 10 reps using moderate weight.

Bent Over Cable Row

Adjust the pulley to a low setting and grab the handle with your right hand.

Bend forward from your waist. Bend your knees.

Put your left hand on your left thigh for balance. Use moderate weight.

Keeping your right arm straight with a slight bend in your right elbow, swing the pulley handle out in an arc and swing your right arm up so it is parallel to the floor, but only swing it out as far as you comfortably can.

Then bring the weight back down to where you began the exercise. After 10 reps with your right arm, repeat with your left arm.

Do one set of 10 reps with your right arm. Switch sides and do another set of 10 reps with your left arm. Switch back to your right arm and do another 10 reps, and finish with 10 more reps with your left arm.

Dumbbell Upright Row

Stand holding a moderate weight dumbbell at your side in your right hand and put your left hand on a support so you will keep balance.

Raise the dumbbell up to your shoulder or as high as you can comfortably. Then lower it to your side where you began the exercise.

Do one set of 10 reps with your right hand. Switch arms and do another set of 10 reps with your left arm. Switch back to your right arm and do another 10 reps, and finish with 10 more reps with your left arm.

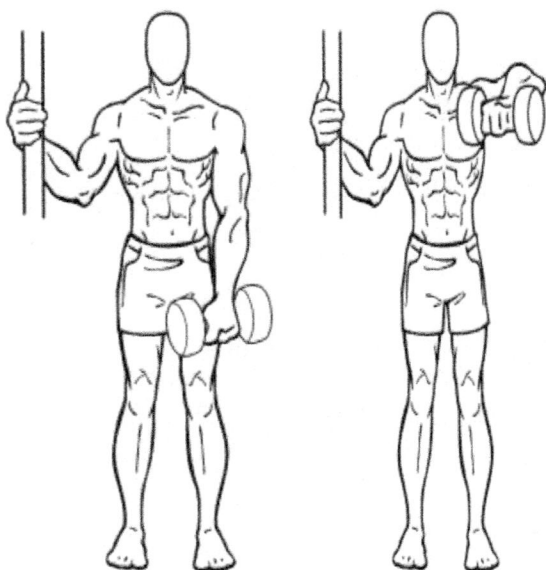

Upright Barbell Row

Using moderate to a light barbell or just the barbell without weights, stand with your feet shoulder width apart with your back straight.

Place your hands shoulder width apart on the barbell and raise it up to your chin in a slow and controlled motion.

Lower in to the starting position in one continuous motion.

Do two sets of 10 reps each.

Core Exercises

Plank in Push Up Position

Place your body in a standard push up position with your toes on the floor and your body raised up.

Hold for 30 seconds (i.e., count from 1 to 30), working your way up to holding this position for two minutes (i.e., a count from 1 to 120).

An easier version: The plank can also be done with your forearms supporting your body instead of your arms.

BASIC CRUNCH SITUPS

Lay on the floor with your back flat and your feet raised up on a bench with your knees bent.

Keep your knees bent at right angles. Place your hands across your chest, or on either side of your head. Avoid pulling on your neck or head to raise yourself up.

Raise your head, shoulders, and chest off the floor and towards your knees, crunching your abdominal muscles. Concentrate on curling up using your upper torso. Lower to the floor and repeat.

Do 2 sets of 20 reps.

Floor Leg Raises

Lie on a floor mat with your hands under your hips to support your back.

With your feet together, raise your straight legs up to a 45-degree angle and pause. Try to keep your lower back flat on the floor as you do these.

Then slowly lower your legs back to the floor where you began the exercise. Repeat.

Do two sets of 10 leg raises each and work up to more if you like.

HIP RAISES – BENT KNEES

Lie on your back and your arms should be straight along the sides of your body.

Begin by bending your knees and raising your feet slightly off the floor.

Keeping your upper back and arms flat on the floor, with your knees bent, raise your hips up and off the floor, so that your knees rise over you as far as you can comfortably.

Drop your hips down to the floor to the starting position. Repeat trying not to let your feet touch the floor and do 10 reps.

Do two sets of 10 reps.

BACK BRIDGE

Lie on your back as shown on the diagram.

Raise your hips off the floor toward the ceiling by pressing both of your heels into the floor and simultaneously raising your hips so that your back and upper body and thighs are in a straight line.

Lower your hips back down to the floor, and as your hips return to the floor, raise your hips back up in a continuous motion.

Do two sets of 10 reps.

273

SIDE PLANK

Lay on your right side with your legs straight preparing to support your body with your right forearm.

Raise up balancing on your forearm and the sides of your feet.

Hold this side plank position for a count of 30, or however long you can hold the side plank position.

Lower yourself, then roll over to your left side and hold the side plank on your left side for a count of 30.

Then roll over to your right side and repeat.

Then finish with for a count of 30 on your left side.

Work up to holding each side plank for 120 seconds or more.

SWISS BALL SIDE BENDS

If possible, have someone hold the Swiss Ball while you do these.

Lie one side of your torso, and with your waist and hip against a Swiss Ball. Position your feet on the floor in a wide stance for support and balance.

Raise your torso up off the ball, then lower yourself back down on the ball. Then raise your torso up in one continuous motion and lower. Repeat 10 times.

Do two sets of 10 reps on each side.

Swiss-Ball Abdominal Pull In

Lie on your stomach as if you are going to do a pushup.

Ask someone to help you place a Swiss-Ball under your knees and shins or put a Swiss-Ball under your knees and shins if you can comfortably do that yourself.

Keeping your back straight, push up with both arms into a raised pushup position.

Pull your knees toward you so the ball goes toward you and under your ankles.

Then extend your legs going back to your original position.

Do two sets of 10 reps each.

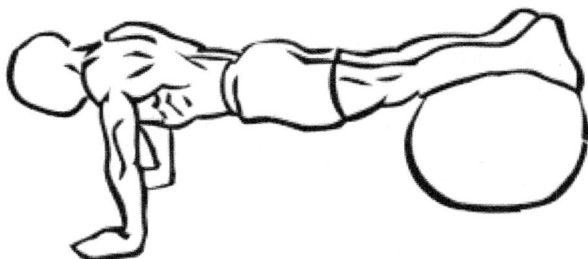

BACK RAISES

Lie flat on your stomach with your arms stretched out in front of you.

Slowly raise your arms and legs simultaneously off the floor, and hold this position for a count of 3, then lower yourself to the floor. Repeat.

Do two sets of 10 reps.

Crunches with Alternating Legs

Place your hands on the sides of your head. Try not to put your hands behind your head as you should not pull on your neck when doing this exercise.

Lie on your back and bring your left elbow up to almost touch your right knee (or crunch up as far as you comfortably can).

Then curl back and bring your right elbow up to try and almost touch your left knee (or crunch up as far as you comfortably can) and curl back. And so on.

Do two sets of 15 reps.

Stretching and Flexibility

Rotator Cuff Muscle Stretch ("Wax On – Wax Off").

Stand upright with your feet apart and place a fully inflated exercise ball at chest height against a wall and hold it against the wall with your left hand. Then roll the ball making 10 circles while pressing the ball against the wall.

Switch arms and repeat and do 10 more complete circles using the opposite arm.

Repeat and do one more set of 10 circles with each arm.

Oblique Stretch

Sit on a gym mat and place your left ankle over your right knee. Place your right elbow on the side of your left knee.

Extend your left arm behind you and gently and slowly turn to the left. Hold for three breaths or about 20 seconds.

Then do the same on the opposite side starting by placing your right ankle over your left knee and hold for three breaths or about 20 seconds.

Oblique and Shoulder Stretch.

In a standing position, extend your arms over your head. Bend your elbows, then place your left hand over your right elbow, and bend to your left as far as you comfortably can and hold for 30 seconds.

Repeat with placing your right hand on your left elbow and bending to the right as far as you comfortably can and hold for 30 seconds.

Stretch Chart

See the Chart on the next page and add any of these stretches.

These 12 stretches should take under 7 minutes to do each day.

The muscle groups being stretched are shown below the diagram of the stretch.

Gastrocnemius and Soleus = Calf muscles

Psoas = Hip Flexor, a core muscle

Hamstring = Posterior thigh muscle

Adductors = Group of muscles around the hip, core muscles

Quadriceps = Front and side thigh muscles. Hold on to a chair for support when doing this stretch.

Gluteals = Buttocks muscles

Triceps = Large back upper arm muscle

Pectorals = Upper chest muscles

Hold each stretch for 20 to 30 seconds.

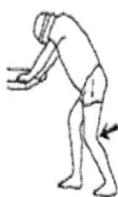

Hamstrings

Gastrocnemius

Soleus

Psoas

Adductors

Adductors

Adductors

Quadriceps

Triceps

Pectorals

Gluteals

291

More on Agility and Flexibility

Daily stretching will help maintain your flexibility. If you want more stretching, flexibility, and agility exercises, our favorite is the large Fitness Blender site at https://www.fitnessblender.com/ where there are several free videos dealing with flexibility and agility.

Cardio Training

Maintaining cardio fitness means you will be less tired during a round of golf. Do cardio on a regular schedule for at least 50 minutes to 1 hour per day, three days a week (do the weights program on the two other days).

Activities like swimming, tennis, walking, cycling, jogging, jumping rope, and using cardio machines are all great choices.

More strenuous cardio activities are doing jumping jacks, and burpees on a High-intensity interval training (HIIT) programs offered for free on the Fitness Blender website.

The most important aspect is having a program and sticking to it.

Most experts (Mayo Clinic, American Heart Association, and others) agree the time spent on a weekly aerobic program should total at least 75 minutes of intense aerobic activity, or 150 minutes of moderate aerobic activity (per week).[35]

If you don't have a cardio program at present, you need to gradually work yourself into a program you can stick with considering your present working and family schedules.

One example of an aerobic program, is the one Greg Norman sticks with. Greg, now in his sixties, works out five times a week.

Greg devotes the first 45 minutes of each session using different cardio machines. This works out to 225 minutes of aerobic excises per week.

Set your own goals and work out your own program with the help and advice of your medical professional. Following a regular weekly fitness program will give you the energy you need on the golf course, as well as in life in general.

Balance Programs

As we age, cells in the vestibular system, which is in the inner ear, die off and balancing becomes more difficult. So, to help you balance better, balancing exercises are important to maintain the vestibular system.[36]

Balance Boards

Start with the easiest balance board and ask the gym staff for a recommendation. Place the Balance Board on the floor. Step onto the board with both feet and try to balance yourself for 15 seconds. Work up to balancing yourself for 2 minutes.

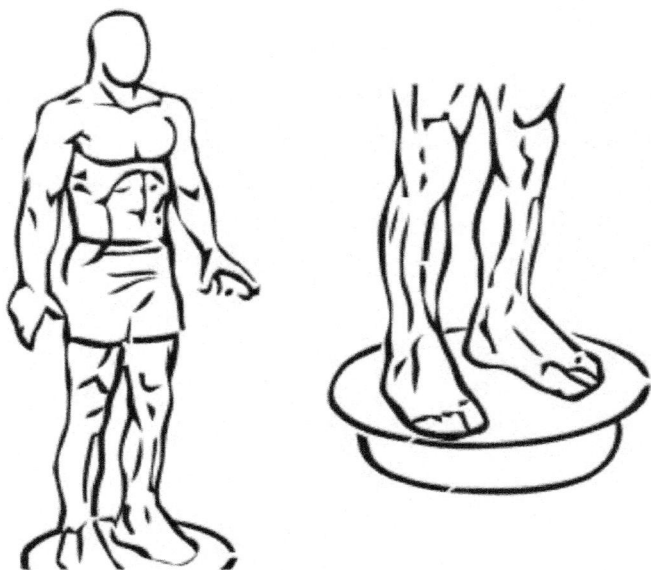

One leg stand.

Using a post or wall for balance stand straight keeping your back straight.

Raise one foot off the ground and behind you while standing on the other leg. Hold for 10 seconds.

Lower your leg and repeat with your other leg for 10 seconds.

Alternate 10 times doing two reps at a time with each leg.

Do a leg stand with each leg 5 times.

Work up to holding each lifted pose for 30 seconds.

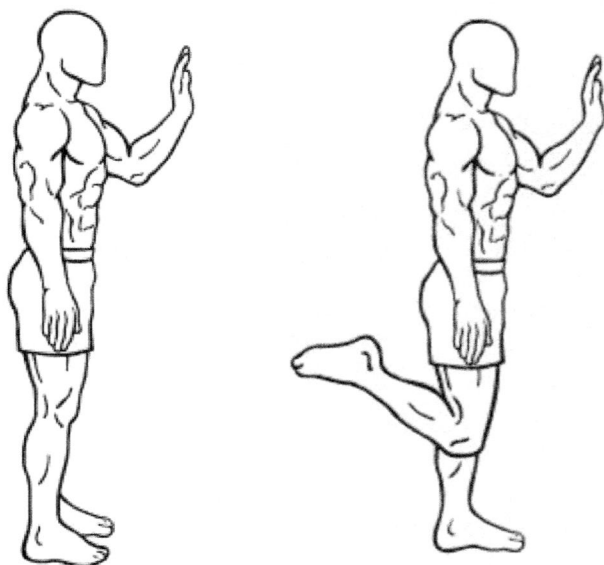

Stork Stance Bicep Curl with Dumbbells

This may be difficult if you haven't done these before. You may be able to do this after doing the preceding balancing exercises for several weeks.

Grasp a pair of lightweight dumbbells in each hand, palms facing up.

Standing on one foot, extend your other foot slightly back at first (work on extending it further back as you become more familiar with this exercise). Allow your arms to hang down, so your arms and the dumbbells are hanging in front of your body.

While on one foot, curl your arms up contracting your biceps.

Work up to two sets of 10 reps with standing on each leg.

Finish a Gym Session With One Brief High Intensity Cardio Exercise

WARNING: If you are unfamiliar with High Intensity Cardio, or if you haven't been finishing Weight Exercise Programs in the gym with brief High Intensity Cardio Exercises, or if you haven't been doing swimming workouts, or haven't been doing strenuous exercises, get medical advice before you do these programs. These programs will increase your heart rate and burn calories.

Do these at your own risk.

After your regular gym routine, do <u>one</u> of these High Intensity Exercises.

Change to different exercises after each gym session, then slowly jog in place for 45 seconds, followed by walking in place for 45 seconds to cool down, or longer until your heart rate decreases.

The suggested number, time periods, etc. to start with are only suggestions. Do the number of reps you feel is appropriate to begin with and set a goal for the amount you want to reach over a 6-week period.

If you are not sure how to do each exercise, ask someone at the gym. These exercises are well known high intensity cardio exercises:

Choice 1: 20 Burpees – work up to 50

Choice 2: 20 Star Jumps – work up to 50

Choice 3: 20 Jumping Jacks – work up to 50

Choice 4: 2 minutes of Mountain Climbers work up to 5 minutes

Choice 5: 20 Squat Jumps – work up to 50

Also, if your medical advisor clears you for a high intensity workout, you may want to try a 30 to 90-minute High Intensity Interval Training YouTube Video to burn a lot of calories.

Swimming Programs

Swimming is beneficial for most people, but it's not for everyone. WARNING: If you have conditions such as heart failure, high blood pressure, asthma or lung problems, deep water may increase the pressure on your heart, increasing blood pressure and exacerbating breathing problems. Only begin a swimming program if you have gotten medical clearance.

Swimming is an ideal workout as you grow older and works all the muscles groups.[37] Some of the additional benefits of a swimming workout are:

- Makes your heart stronger
- Lowers blood pressure
- Improves circulation
- Easy on the joints
- Improves bone mineral density
- Increases flexibility and improves posture
- Helps alleviate back pain
- Tones your muscles
- Reduces stress[38]

There are many swimming workouts for seniors which you can find on the internet which range from doing a few laps and resting, to a full one hour 2500-meter workout using various strokes and equipment. Here's a sample of a swimming workout for beginners.

Senior Swim Workout

Do the freestyle or crawl for the swimming stroke in this workout. You can change to breaststroke or backstroke if you like.

Assuming the pool is 25 meters long, begin with slowly swimming freestyle for four lengths (100 meters) with a rest after each length (if you need to rest).

Next, swim up and back (50 meters) 4 times and rest after every 50 meters. Pick up the pace to where you are comfortable. Remember to rest after each lap, or rest after doing a length if you need to.

Next, swim up and back (50 meters) 4 times at a slow pace resting when you want to rest.

Next sprint 4 X 25 meters. Rest before beginning the sprint on each length and catch your breath before beginning the next length.

Next, Swim easily up and back (50 meters), resting after each lap.

Total distance 700 meters.

Do this Beginner Swim Workout 3 days a week. Remember to take rest breaks as often as needed.

Other Programs Your Gym Offers

If your gym offers aerobic classes or other classes that interest you, try out a class. The first time you attend a class, you may feel awkward, but most everyone feels that way and has gone through it themselves.

Take your cardio workouts outdoors. Studies have determined people who exercise outdoors are more energized and less frustrated. Walk, jog, bike, run, or any exercise activity, and see how you feel compared to an indoor gym workout.

Join an outdoor boot camp exercise group.

Don't get discouraged. Simply know there are good days and bad days to everything you do. Variety will keep you fresh.

Join a Pilates class that will improve your flexibility and core muscles. Core muscles are extremely important to the golfer.

A yoga course will help you stretch and help you maintain flexibility for your golf swing. Tai Chi does this as well.

10. YOU ARE ON YOUR WAY

"The best thing about tomorrow is, I will be better than today. I will be a better golfer, person, father, husband, and friend. That's what's best about and the beauty of tomorrow."

- Tiger Woods

It's all very simple. To reach and maintain your full golf potential requires a regular schedule to accomplish your goals. Regularly doing something gives benefits much more than occasionally doing something. Here is a plan of action to follow right now:

Starting today, schedule a weekly practice session when you can practice the golf drills, techniques and tips set out in Chapters 2, 4 and 5.

Look at your diet and decide today on changing to a healthy diet where you will be consuming less calories than you expend daily. Consuming less calories and increasing exercise will make you play better, and be a more fit and attractive person.

Plan a date to play the game of "Snake" or "Wolf" explained in the fun golf formats in Chapter 8.

Plan and schedule time to exercise in accordance with the exercise programs in Chapter 9. Start with two weight sessions per week and three cardio sessions per week.

If you plan and stick to it, you will reach your full golf playing potential and enjoy golf and life a lot more. Don't get discouraged if you don't follow your plan now and then. Having at least a regular plan is better than not having a plan at all.

Mark Twain joked about procrastination when he said, "Don't leave things until tomorrow, what may be done the day after tomorrow just the same."

Instead of procrastination, think about the Chinese philosopher Laozi's proverb, "The longest journey begins with a single step."

So, start today, or tomorrow, and do something good for yourself to improve, become a better golfer, and a more fit, healthy, and attractive person by following the programs in this book.

It takes time to adjust to a new healthy and enjoyable way of life. If you fall off the schedule, get back right on it again. And set goals for yourself.

How to Set Realistic Goals For Yourself

There are three aspects in setting goals for yourself that are very important:

1. Plan out specific goals for yourself. Just telling yourself you will work out is not enough. Taking action by scheduling time for two gym sessions for weight training per week for a period of two months is a definite specific goal you will more likely follow.[39]

2. Don't make the goal an easy one. Make the goal a bit difficult.[40]

3. Finally, consider the reward you will receive if you reach your goal, e.g., a more attractive and fit body, a better golfer, more respect from associates, etc.[41]

Gabriel Garcia Marquez said, "It's not true people stop pursuing dreams because they grow old. They grow old because they stop pursuing their dreams."

And, keep a strong will as Christopher Reeve said, "So many of our dreams at first seem impossible, then they seem improbable, and then, when we summon the will, they soon become inevitable."

Thank you for reading this book and let us know how you progress. Contact us through our website www.TeamGolfwell.com.

Appendix: Journal for Tracking Your Golf Work Outs

Date: _____

Body Weight: _____

Exercise   Sets   # of Reps

_____

_____

_____

_____

_____

_____

_____

_____

_____

Comments:

_____

_____

Date: _____

Body Weight: _____

Exercise   Sets   # of Reps

_____

_____

_____

_____

_____

_____

_____

_____

_____

_____

Comments:

_____

_____

Date: _____

Body Weight: _____

Exercise   Sets   # of Reps

_____

_____

_____

_____

_____

_____

_____

_____

_____

Comments:

_____

_____

Date: _____

Body Weight: _____

Exercise   Sets   # of Reps

_____

_____

_____

_____

_____

_____

_____

_____

_____

_____

Comments:

_____

_____

Date: _____

Body Weight: _____

Exercise   Sets   # of Reps

_____

_____

_____

_____

_____

_____

_____

_____

_____

_____

Comments:

_____

_____

Date: _____

Body Weight: _____

Exercise   Sets   # of Reps

_____

_____

_____

_____

_____

_____

_____

_____

_____

_____

Comments:

_____

_____

Date: _____

Body Weight: _____

Exercise   Sets   # of Reps

_____

_____

_____

_____

_____

_____

_____

_____

_____

Comments:

_____

_____

Date: _____

Body Weight: _____

Exercise   Sets   # of Reps

_____

_____

_____

_____

_____

_____

_____

_____

_____

_____

Comments:

_____

_____

Date: _____

Body Weight: _____

Exercise   Sets   # of Reps

_____

_____

_____

_____

_____

_____

_____

_____

_____

_____

Comments:

_____

_____

Date: _____

Body Weight: _____

Exercise   Sets   # of Reps

_____

_____

_____

_____

_____

_____

_____

_____

_____

_____

Comments:

_____

_____

Date: _____

Body Weight: _____

Exercise   Sets   # of Reps

_____

_____

_____

_____

_____

_____

_____

_____

_____

_____

Comments:

_____

_____

Date: _____

Body Weight: _____

Exercise   Sets   # of Reps

_____

_____

_____

_____

_____

_____

_____

_____

_____

_____

Comments:

_____

_____

Date: _____

Body Weight: _____

Exercise   Sets   # of Reps

_____

_____

_____

_____

_____

_____

_____

_____

_____

Comments:

_____

_____

Date: _____

Body Weight: _____

Exercise   Sets   # of Reps

_____

_____

_____

_____

_____

_____

_____

_____

_____

_____

Comments:

_____

_____

Date: _____

Body Weight: _____

Exercise   Sets   # of Reps

_____

_____

_____

_____

_____

_____

_____

_____

_____

_____

Comments:

_____

_____

Date: _____

Body Weight: _____

Exercise   Sets   # of Reps

_____

_____

_____

_____

_____

_____

_____

_____

_____

_____

Comments:

_____

_____

Date: _____

Body Weight: _____

Exercise   Sets   # of Reps

_____

_____

_____

_____

_____

_____

_____

_____

_____

_____

Comments:

_____

_____

Reach Your Full Playing Potential and Have Fun Doing It

Date: _____

Body Weight: _____

Exercise   Sets   # of Reps

_____

_____

_____

_____

_____

_____

_____

_____

_____

_____

Comments:

_____

_____

Date: _____

Body Weight: _____

Exercise   Sets   # of Reps

_____

_____

_____

_____

_____

_____

_____

_____

_____

_____

Comments:

_____

_____

Date: _____

Body Weight: _____

Exercise   Sets   # of Reps

_____

_____

_____

_____

_____

_____

_____

_____

_____

Comments:

_____

_____

Date: _____

Body Weight: _____

Exercise   Sets   # of Reps

_____

_____

_____

_____

_____

_____

_____

_____

_____

_____

Comments:

_____

_____

Date: _____

Body Weight: _____

Exercise   Sets   # of Reps

_____

_____

_____

_____

_____

_____

_____

_____

_____

_____

Comments:

_____

_____

Date: _____

Body Weight: _____

Exercise   Sets   # of Reps

_____

_____

_____

_____

_____

_____

_____

_____

_____

Comments:

_____

_____

Date: _____

Body Weight: _____

Exercise   Sets   # of Reps

_____

_____

_____

_____

_____

_____

_____

_____

_____

_____

Comments:

_____

_____

Date: _____

Body Weight: _____

Exercise   Sets   # of Reps

_____

_____

_____

_____

_____

_____

_____

_____

_____

_____

Comments:

_____

_____

Date: _____

Body Weight: _____

Exercise   Sets   # of Reps

_____

_____

_____

_____

_____

_____

_____

_____

_____

Comments:

_____

_____

Date: _____

Body Weight: _____

Exercise   Sets   # of Reps

_____

_____

_____

_____

_____

_____

_____

_____

_____

Comments:

_____

_____

Date: _____

Body Weight: _____

Exercise   Sets   # of Reps

_____

_____

_____

_____

_____

_____

_____

_____

_____

_____

Comments:

_____

_____

Date: _____

Body Weight: _____

Exercise   Sets   # of Reps

_____

_____

_____

_____

_____

_____

_____

_____

_____

_____

Comments:

_____

_____

Date: _____

Body Weight: _____

Exercise   Sets   # of Reps

_____

_____

_____

_____

_____

_____

_____

_____

_____

_____

Comments:

_____

_____

Date: _____

Body Weight: _____

Exercise   Sets   # of Reps

_____

_____

_____

_____

_____

_____

_____

_____

_____

_____

Comments:

_____

_____

Date: _____

Body Weight: _____

Exercise	Sets	# of Reps

_____

_____

_____

_____

_____

_____

_____

_____

_____

_____

Comments:

_____

_____

Date: _____

Body Weight: _____

Exercise   Sets   # of Reps

_____

_____

_____

_____

_____

_____

_____

_____

_____

_____

Comments:

_____

_____

Date: _____

Body Weight: _____

Exercise   Sets   # of Reps

_____

_____

_____

_____

_____

_____

_____

_____

_____

_____

Comments:

_____

_____

Date: _____

Body Weight: _____

Exercise   Sets   # of Reps

_____

_____

_____

_____

_____

_____

_____

_____

_____

Comments:

_____

_____

Date: _____

Body Weight: _____

Exercise   Sets   # of Reps

_____

_____

_____

_____

_____

_____

_____

_____

_____

_____

Comments:

_____

_____

Date: _____

Body Weight: _____

Exercise   Sets   # of Reps

_____

_____

_____

_____

_____

_____

_____

_____

_____

_____

Comments:

_____

_____

Date: _____

Body Weight: _____

Exercise   Sets   # of Reps

_____

_____

_____

_____

_____

_____

_____

_____

_____

_____

Comments:

_____

_____

Date: _____

Body Weight: _____

Exercise   Sets   # of Reps

_____

_____

_____

_____

_____

_____

_____

_____

_____

Comments:

_____

_____

Date: _____

Body Weight: _____

Exercise   Sets   # of Reps

_____

_____

_____

_____

_____

_____

_____

_____

_____

_____

Comments:

_____

_____

Date: _____

Body Weight: _____

Exercise   Sets   # of Reps

_____

_____

_____

_____

_____

_____

_____

_____

_____

Comments:

_____

_____

Date: _____

Body Weight: _____

Exercise   Sets   # of Reps

_____

_____

_____

_____

_____

_____

_____

_____

_____

_____

Comments:

_____

_____

Date: _____

Body Weight: _____

Exercise   Sets   # of Reps

_____

_____

_____

_____

_____

_____

_____

_____

_____

Comments:

_____

_____

Date: _____

Body Weight: _____

Exercise   Sets   # of Reps

_____

_____

_____

_____

_____

_____

_____

_____

_____

Comments:

_____

_____

Date: _____

Body Weight: _____

Exercise   Sets   # of Reps

_____

_____

_____

_____

_____

_____

_____

_____

_____

_____

Comments:

_____

_____

Date: _____

Body Weight: _____

Exercise   Sets   # of Reps

_____

_____

_____

_____

_____

_____

_____

_____

_____

_____

Comments:

_____

_____

Date: _____

Body Weight: _____

Exercise   Sets   # of Reps

_____

_____

_____

_____

_____

_____

_____

_____

_____

_____

Comments:

_____

_____

Date: _____

Body Weight: _____

Exercise   Sets   # of Reps

_____

_____

_____

_____

_____

_____

_____

_____

_____

_____

Comments:

_____

_____

Date: _____

Body Weight: _____

Exercise　　　　Sets　　# of Reps

_____

_____

_____

_____

_____

_____

_____

_____

_____

_____

Comments:

_____

_____

Date: _____

Body Weight: _____

Exercise   Sets   # of Reps

_____

_____

_____

_____

_____

_____

_____

_____

_____

Comments:

_____

_____

Date: _____

Body Weight: _____

Exercise   Sets   # of Reps

_____

_____

_____

_____

_____

_____

_____

_____

_____

_____

Comments:

_____

_____

Date: _____

Body Weight: _____

Exercise   Sets   # of Reps

_____

_____

_____

_____

_____

_____

_____

_____

_____

_____

Comments:

_____

_____

Date: _____

Body Weight: _____

Exercise   Sets   # of Reps

_____

_____

_____

_____

_____

_____

_____

_____

_____

_____

Comments:

_____

_____

Date: _____

Body Weight: _____

Exercise　　　　Sets　　# of Reps

_____

_____

_____

_____

_____

_____

_____

_____

_____

Comments:

_____

_____

Date: _____

Body Weight: _____

Exercise   Sets   # of Reps

_____

_____

_____

_____

_____

_____

_____

_____

_____

_____

Comments:

_____

_____

_____

_____

Date: _____

Body Weight: _____

Exercise   Sets   # of Reps

_____

_____

_____

_____

_____

_____

_____

_____

Comments:

_____

_____

Date: _____

Body Weight: _____

Exercise   Sets   # of Reps

_____

_____

_____

_____

_____

_____

_____

_____

_____

_____

Comments:

_____

_____

Date: _____

Body Weight: _____

Exercise   Sets   # of Reps

_____

_____

_____

_____

_____

_____

_____

_____

_____

_____

Comments:

_____

_____

Date: _____

Body Weight: _____

Exercise   Sets   # of Reps

_____

_____

_____

_____

_____

_____

_____

_____

_____

Comments:

_____

_____

Date: _____

Body Weight: _____

Exercise   Sets   # of Reps

_____

_____

_____

_____

_____

_____

_____

_____

_____

Comments:

_____

_____

Date: _____

Body Weight: _____

Exercise   Sets   # of Reps

_____

_____

_____

_____

_____

_____

_____

_____

_____

_____

Comments:

_____

_____

Date: _____

Body Weight: _____

Exercise   Sets   # of Reps

_____

_____

_____

_____

_____

_____

_____

_____

_____

_____

Comments:

_____

_____

Date: _____

Body Weight: _____

Exercise   Sets   # of Reps

_____

_____

_____

_____

_____

_____

_____

_____

_____

_____

Comments:

_____

_____

Date: _____

Body Weight: _____

Exercise   Sets   # of Reps

_____

_____

_____

_____

_____

_____

_____

_____

_____

_____

Comments:

_____

_____

Date: _____

Body Weight: _____

Exercise   Sets   # of Reps

_____

_____

_____

_____

_____

_____

_____

_____

_____

_____

Comments:

_____

_____

Date: _____

Body Weight: _____

Exercise   Sets   # of Reps

_____

_____

_____

_____

_____

_____

_____

_____

_____

_____

Comments:

_____

_____

Date: _____

Body Weight: _____

Exercise   Sets   # of Reps

_____

_____

_____

_____

_____

_____

_____

_____

_____

_____

Comments:

_____

_____

Date: _____

Body Weight: _____

Exercise   Sets   # of Reps

_____

_____

_____

_____

_____

_____

_____

_____

_____

_____

Comments:

_____

_____

Date: _____

Body Weight: _____

Exercise   Sets   # of Reps

_____

_____

_____

_____

_____

_____

_____

_____

_____

Comments:

_____

_____

Date: _____

Body Weight: _____

Exercise   Sets   # of Reps

_____

_____

_____

_____

_____

_____

_____

_____

_____

_____

Comments:

_____

_____

Date: _____

Body Weight: _____

Exercise   Sets   # of Reps

_____

_____

_____

_____

_____

_____

_____

_____

_____

_____

Comments:

_____

_____

Date: _____

Body Weight: _____

Exercise   Sets   # of Reps

_____

_____

_____

_____

_____

_____

_____

_____

_____

_____

Comments:

_____

_____

Date: _____

Body Weight: _____

Exercise   Sets   # of Reps

_____

_____

_____

_____

_____

_____

_____

_____

_____

Comments:

_____

_____

Date: _____

Body Weight: _____

Exercise   Sets   # of Reps

_____

_____

_____

_____

_____

_____

_____

_____

_____

Comments:

_____

_____

Date: _____

Body Weight: _____

Exercise   Sets   # of Reps

_____

_____

_____

_____

_____

_____

_____

_____

_____

_____

Comments:

_____

_____

Date: _____

Body Weight: _____

Exercise   Sets   # of Reps

_____

_____

_____

_____

_____

_____

_____

_____

_____

_____

Comments:

_____

_____

Date: _____

Body Weight: _____

Exercise   Sets   # of Reps

_____

_____

_____

_____

_____

_____

_____

_____

_____

Comments:

_____

_____

Date: _____

Body Weight: _____

Exercise   Sets   # of Reps

_____

_____

_____

_____

_____

_____

_____

_____

_____

_____

Comments:

_____

_____

Date: _____

Body Weight: _____

Exercise   Sets   # of Reps

_____

_____

_____

_____

_____

_____

_____

_____

_____

Comments:

_____

_____

Date: _____

Body Weight: _____

Exercise   Sets   # of Reps

_____

_____

_____

_____

_____

_____

_____

_____

_____

_____

Comments:

_____

_____

Date: _____

Body Weight: _____

Exercise   Sets   # of Reps

_____

_____

_____

_____

_____

_____

_____

_____

_____

_____

Comments:

_____

_____

Date: _____

Body Weight: _____

Exercise   Sets   # of Reps

_____

_____

_____

_____

_____

_____

_____

_____

_____

Comments:

_____

_____

Date: _____

Body Weight: _____

Exercise   Sets   # of Reps

_____

_____

_____

_____

_____

_____

_____

_____

_____

_____

Comments:

_____

_____

Date: _____

Body Weight: _____

Exercise   Sets   # of Reps

_____

_____

_____

_____

_____

_____

_____

_____

_____

_____

Comments:

_____

_____

Date: _____

Body Weight: _____

Exercise   Sets   # of Reps

_____

_____

_____

_____

_____

_____

_____

_____

_____

_____

Comments:

_____

_____

Date: _____

Body Weight: _____

Exercise   Sets   # of Reps

_____

_____

_____

_____

_____

_____

_____

_____

_____

Comments:

_____

_____

Date: _____

Body Weight: _____

Exercise   Sets   # of Reps

_____

_____

_____

_____

_____

_____

_____

_____

_____

Comments:

_____

_____

A final message to you from The Team at Golfwell:

Thank you for reading this book and we hope it helps your game, and best to you! We hope this book will make golf more enjoyable for you.

Above all, have fun playing golf and enjoy all your adventures!

If you liked our book, please take a moment and give it a review. Thank you!

Bruce@teamgolfwell.com

Other books by Team Golfwell are here >
https://www.amazon.com/The-Team-at-Golfwell/e/B01CFW4EQG

Chapter 1

[1] The University of Edinburgh News, "Golf's Many Benefits Brought to the Fore in Health Study," https://www.ed.ac.uk/news/2016/golf-s-many-benefits-brought-to-the-fore-in-health

[2] Ibid.

[3] The Telegraph News, "Playing golf can add five years to your life," http://www.telegraph.co.uk/news/2016/10/06/playing-golf-can-add-five-years-to-your-life-according-to-resear/

[4] The West Australian News, "Scientists Say People Who Play Golf Live Longer," https://thewest.com.au/news/australia/scientists-say-people-who-play-golf-tend-to-live-longer-ng-b88587212z

[5] Ibid.

[6] Ibid.

The Cleveland Clinic, "Build Muscles, Lose Weight by Adding Strength Training to Your Workout" https://health.clevelandclinic.org/2016/10/build-muscles-lose-weight-by-adding-strength-training-to-your-workout/

[7] Vision, "The Future of Golf – Fore Health Play Golf," http://thefutureofgolf.eu/fore-health/

[8] Ibid.

[9] GALLUP, Analytics Consultant, responding to our email enquiry on what most people feel is most important in life.

Chapter 3

[10] Dorothy Lucardie, "The Impact of Fun and Enjoyment on Adult's Learning," https://www.sciencedirect.com/science/article/pii/S1877042814046242

[11] The Mayo Clinic Staff, "Stress Relief from Laughter? It's No Joke," https://www.mayoclinic.org/healthy-lifestyle/stress-management/in-depth/stress-relief/art-20044456

[12] LOU University, "Why Laughter Is Good for Mental Health, Breaks the Cycle of Psychological Negativity" http://www.laughteronlineuniversity.com/laughter-good-mental-health/

[13] The Mayo Clinic Staff, "Stress Relief from Laughter? It's No Joke," https://www.mayoclinic.org/healthy-lifestyle/stress-management/in-depth/stress-relief/art-20044456

[14] LOU University, "Why Laughter Is Good for Mental Health, Breaks the Cycle of Psychological Negativity" http://www.laughteronlineuniversity.com/laughter-good-mental-health/

[15] J. Yim, "Therapeutic Benefits of Laughter in Mental Health: A Theoretical Review" https://www.ncbi.nlm.nih.gov/pubmed/27439375

[16] Ibid.

[17] Twiinsane, "Bradley Cooper Can't Stop Laughing," https://www.youtube.com/watch?v=b28_wgzR34Y

---

[18] Psychology Today, "The Benefits of Laughter," https://www.psychologytoday.com/articles/200304/the-benefits-laughter

Chapter 4

[19] Mayo Clinic Staff, "Osteoarthritis," https://www.mayoclinic.org/diseases-conditions/osteoarthritis/diagnosis-treatment/drc-20351930

[20] Healthline, "Understanding Cartilage, Joints, and the Aging Process," https://www.healthline.com/health/osteoarthritis/understanding-aging-and-joints

Chapter 5

[21] Team Golfwell, "Golf Driving Techniques from Golfing Greats and Stories: Proven Golf Driving Techniques from Dustin Johnson, Rory, Jason Day, Justin Thomas, Bubba Watson, and many more," https://www.amazon.com/Driving-Techniques-Golfing-Greats-Stories-ebook/dp/B06XJGY992

[22] Jinhua Guan and Michael G. Wade, "The Effect of Aging on Adaptive Eye-Hand Coordination,"

[23] Brenna Davis, "Age Affecting Flexibility," https://healthyliving.azcentral.com/age-affecting-flexibility-3978.html

[24] Healthline, "Can I Improve My Eye-Hand Coordination?" https://www.healthline.com/health/hand-eye-coordination

[25] Golf Analytics, "An Aging Curve for Putting," https://golfanalytics.wordpress.com/2014/03/13/an-aging-curve-for-putting/

[26] Jack Nicklaus, "Jack Nicklaus on the Three Tee Concept," https://www.youtube.com/watch?time_continue=38&v=R7XV_xlaNgc

[27] Jack Nicklaus Golf Ball Buying Guide, March 2016, http://www.ebay.com/gds/Jack-Nicklaus-Golf-Ball-Buying-Guide-/10000000178722269/g.html

Chapter 7

[28] Helpguide.org, "Senior Exercise and Fitness Tips" https://www.helpguide.org/articles/healthy-living/exercise-and-fitness-as-you-age.htm

[29] American Heart Association, "The American Heart Association's Diet and Lifestyle Recommendations," http://www.heart.org/HEARTORG/HealthyLiving/HealthyEating/Nutrition/The-American-Heart-Associations-Diet-and-Lifestyle-Recommendations_UCM_305855_Article.jsp#.WjgHp0qWZpk

[30] Ibid.

Chapter 8

[31] Golf Player Demographic Statistics, https://www.statisticbrain.com/golf-player-demographic-statistics/

[32] Team Golfwell has a 4-book series of adult golf jokes: see our website for details on these books, and others if you are interested https://www.teamgolfwell.com/.

[33] Phil Mickleson's Secrets of the Short Game Part I, https://www.youtube.com/watch?v=GhzY7TIMnMU

Chapter 9

34 University of Florida News, "Adding Variety to An Exercise Routine Helps Increase Adherence," http://news.ufl.edu/archive/2000/10/adding-variety-to-an-exercise-routine-helps-increase-adherence.html

35 Mayo Clinic Staff, "How Much Exercise Does the Average Adult need," https://www.mayoclinic.org/healthy-lifestyle/fitness/expert-answers/exercise/faq-20057916; American Heart Association, "American Heart Association Recommendations for Physical Activity in Adults," http://www.heart.org/HEARTORG/HealthyLiving/PhysicalActivity/FitnessBasics/American-Heart-Association-Recommendations-for-Physical-Activity-in-Adults_UCM_307976_Article.jsp#.WjmuJN-WZpk

36 Dr. Anthony Komaroff, Harvard Medical School - In Association with Harvard Health Publications, "Why does balance decline with age?" https://www.askdoctork.com/why-does-balance-decline-with-age-201306054928

37 American Senior Activities, "Health Benefits of Swimming for Seniors," http://www.ascseniorcare.com/swimming-for-seniors/

38 Ibid.

Chapter 10

39 Seth J. Gillihan, Ph.D., "3 Ways to Craft Compelling Goals", Psychology Today, https://www.psychologytoday.com/blog/think-act-be/201611/3-ways-craft-compelling-goals

40 Ibid.

41 Ibid.

Printed in Great Britain
by Amazon